Davidson Titles

D1604654

7-10-98

THE CULT OF THE
HEDGEHOG

DENNIS KELSEY-WOOD

TS-280

Contents

Photography by Ralph Lermayer

© 1997 by T.F.H. Publications, Inc.

Distributed in the UNITED STATES to the Pet Trade by T.F.H. Publications, Inc., One T.F.H. Plaza, Neptune City, NJ 07753; distributed in the UNITED STATES to the Bookstore and Library Trade by National Book Network, Inc. 4720 Boston Way, Lanham MD 20706; in CANADA to the Pet Trade by H & L Pet Supplies Inc., 27 Kingston Crescent, Kitchener, Ontario N2B 2T6; Rolf C. Hagen Inc., 3225 Sartelon St. Laurent-Montreal Quebec H4R 1E8; in CANADA to the Book Trade by Vanwell Publishing Ltd., 1 Northrup Crescent, St. Catharines, Ontario L2M 6P5 ; in ENGLAND by T.F.H. Publications, PO Box 15, Waterlooville PO7 6BQ; in AUSTRALIA AND THE SOUTH PACIFIC by T.F.H. (Australia), Pty. Ltd., Box 149, Brookvale 2100 N.S.W., Australia; in NEW ZEALAND by Brooklands Aquarium Ltd. 5 McGiven Drive, New Plymouth, RD1 New Zealand; in Japan by T.F.H. Publications, Japan—Jiro Tsuda, 10-12-3 Ohjidai, Sakura, Chiba 285, Japan; in SOUTH AFRICA by Lopis (Pty) Ltd., P.O. Box 39127, Booysens, 2016, Johannesburg, South Africa. Published by T.F.H. Publications, Inc.
MANUFACTURED IN THE
UNITED STATES OF AMERICA
BY T.F.H. PUBLICATIONS, INC.

CUSTOMARY U.S. MEASURES AND EQUIVALENTS	METRIC MEASURES AND EQUIVALENTS

LENGTH

1 inch (in)		= 2.54 cm	1 millimeter (mm)		= .0394 in
1 foot (ft)	= 12 in	= .3048 m	1 centimeter (cm)	= 10 mm	= .3937 in
I yard (yd)	= 3 ft	= .9144 m	1 meter (m)	= 1000 mm	= 1.0936 yd
1 mile (mi)	= 1760 yd	= 1.6093 km	1 kilometer (km)	= 1000 m	= .6214 mi
1 nautical mile	= 1.152 mi	= 1.853 km			

AREA

1 square inch (in²)		= 6.4516 cm²	1 sq centimeter (cm²)	= 100 mm²	= .155 in²
1 square foot (ft²)	= 144 in²	= .093 m²	1 sq meter (m²)	= 10,000 cm²	= 1.196 yd²
1 square yard (yd²)	= 9 ft²	= .8361 m²	1 hectare (ha)	= 10,000 m²	= 2.4711 acres
1 acre	= 4840 yd²	= 4046.86 m²	1 sq kilometer (km²)	= 100 ha	= .3861 mi²
1 square mile(mi²)	= 640 acre	= 2.59 km²			

WEIGHT

1 ounce (oz)	= 437.5 grains	= 28.35 g	1 milligram (mg)	= .0154 grain	
1 pound (lb)	= 16 oz	= .4536 kg	1 gram (g)	= 1000 mg	= .0353 oz
1 short ton	= 2000 lb	= .9072 t	1 kilogram (kg)	= 1000 g	= 2.2046 lb
1 long ton	= 2240 lb	= 1.0161 t	1 tonne (t)	= 1000 kg	= 1.1023 short tons
			1 tonne		= .9842 long ton

VOLUME

1 cubic inch (in³)		= 16.387 cm³	1 cubic centimeter (cm³)		= .061 in³
1 cubic foot (ft³)	= 1728 in³	= .028 m³	1 cubic decimeter (dm³)	= 1000 cm³	= .353 ft³
1 cubic yard (yd³)	= 27 ft³	= .7646 m³	1 cubic meter (m³)	= 1000 dm³	= 1.3079 yd³
			1 liter (l)	= 1 dm³	= .2642 gal
1 fluid ounce (fl oz)		= 2.957 cl	1 hectoliter (hl)	= 100 l	= 2.8378 bu
1 liquid pint (pt)	= 16 fl oz	= .4732 l			
1 liquid quart (qt)	= 2 pt	= .946 l			
1 gallon (gal)	= 4 qt	= 3.7853 l			
1 dry pint		= .5506 l			
1 bushel (bu)	= 64 dry pt	= 35.2381 l			

TEMPERATURE

CELSIUS° = 5/9 (F° − 32°)   FAHRENHEIT° = 9/5 C° + 32°

Preface

The hedgehog hobby, though still in its infancy, continues to expand. When I wrote *African Pygmy Hedgehogs As Your New Pet*, the amount of data devoted exclusively to these pets was very limited. Since that time, new information has been gained at an increasing rate.

Further, when I served as director of the North American Hedgehog Association (NAHA), I was fortunate enough to receive many hundreds of letters from hedgehog owners in which they stated their problems, as well as areas of the book cited which they would have liked to see expanded.

This book answers many of the questions that I have been asked, while its larger extent allows more space to discuss subjects in greater detail.

My many hedgehog friends and fellow breeders have been most helpful in providing food for thought, as well as factual infor-

mation relative to their stock. I am indebted to them for their material and moral support. A special thank you goes to my wife Eve and son Alexander for their hard work and help with our own small herd.

I also thank the following people whose own writings I have freely drawn upon and who have helped to advance the frontiers of this hobby: Dawn Wrobel, Kirsten Kranz, Chris Staley, DVM, Anthony Smith, DVM, Pat Storer, Professor Edmund D. Brodie, Jr., and Dick Brisky.

To Professor Edmund D. Brodie, Jr., of Utah State University, I am especially grateful for reading the manuscript and graciously providing the foreword to this book. Finally, I thank my publisher, Dr. Herbert R. Axelrod, and his managing editor, Neal Pronek, for the editorial freedom they have always blessed upon me over many years of working with them.

Foreword

This book on African pygmy hedgehogs should prove valuable to the serious hobbyist as well as to those who have recently fallen under the spell of this delightful little creature. The knowledge of proper husbandry has increased enormously since I started a small breeding colony some 20 years ago. I find the advances in knowledge exciting and well presented by the author, who obviously cares deeply about hedgehogs.

These are pets that are only a relatively small number of generations away from wild animals, and I was pleased to see behaviors described that I have observed in wild individuals in Africa. Even in some large cities, it was possible to locate hedgehogs at night by listening for the squealing and snorting of a mating pair.

I would add that one should always turn on a light when getting out of bed at night if your pets are allowed to roam freely in the house. It probably does a hedgehog no great harm to be stepped on or kicked, but it can be very exciting to the pet owner.

Professor Edmund D. Brodie, Jr.
Head of the Department of
Biology, Utah State University
May 1995

Hedgehogs' calm, serene manner and ease of maintenance make them a popular pet with older folks.

Introduction

Exotic animals, of which the hedgehog is but one, are not a new pet phenomenon. People have always been interested in the unusual, even the bizarre, but few of these creatures ever gain the sort of following that makes them a major household pet. The first really definable group of exotics to attain great popularity were the many foreign birds—parrots, softbills, and finches—that started to appear during the late 1800s. From their ranks came the ubiquitous budgerigar, lovebirds, the gray parrot, the Amazons, zebra finches, and mynah birds, to name but a few.

These were to be followed by tropical fish such as guppies, platys, and tetras, all of which are popular examples. A select few mammals, such as the guinea pig, hamster, and gerbil gained house-hold status before there was a

These small mammals are specially equipped to teach children to handle them gently.

shift to reptiles and amphibians. In recent years these have been the main thrust of popular exotics.

During the late 1980s a new mammal suddenly burst onto the pet scene. By any standard it was unusual because it was a pig, á la the potbellied variety. It took America by storm. Although its reign as King of the Exotics was relatively short-lived, it heralded the birth of a shift in animal group popularity. The mammals may well prove to be the new "top dogs" in exotics during the next decade or so. From their ranks, just one or two may well gain the sort of popularity that establishes them as firm household favorites, along with dogs, cats, rabbits, mice, and the other mammals already mentioned earlier.

Even while the potbelly was lord of its domain, another little mam-mal was developing in the wings. Like the potbelly, it is also an unusual critter. It has the poten-tial to become the most popular pet mammal to arrive on the pet scene since the hamster about 50 years ago. It has all the creden-tials to make it a "stayer," around which an enormous hobby is already developing.

The new King of the Exotics is the African pygmy hedgehog, which has the scientific name of *Atelerix albiventris.* It is a ball of prickly spines that Europeans and those people of Africa and Asia are very familiar with. But in the USA, where it is not indigenous, it was perceived to be a miniature porcupine-type of animal. In reality, it is not in any way related to a porcupine.

Like potbellied pigs, hedgehogs (there are a number of species) have been kept in zoos around the world for many years. They are not the most active, eye-catching animals as exhibits, so it is not surprising that they attracted little attention.

However, in the early 1990s a number of the African species were imported into Florida. Of these, the so-called pygmy hedgehog began to gain attention as being cute, pretty and a quite delightful little pet. Even so it achieved only limited success, and at modest prices. Things really changed when a number of exotic breeders, notably Pat Storer, looking to diversify their range of "stock items," happened on the hedgehog.

Very soon, speculative animal investors recognized that here was a pet with a special appeal. Prices started to soar upward as the demand outstripped the supply. Within a few months, animal gold fever had taken over. Hedgehogs were commanding prices of up to four thousand dollars a pair. They started to receive tremendous magazine exposure, this perpetuating the situation.

The big dollar prices were short-lived, though some breeders did make substantial sums of money during this period. By 1994 there were so many breeders churning out these little pets that prices started to fall dramatically. Sadly, a lot of people had borrowed money to invest in breeding pairs thinking the prices would stay high for a long period. This was never going to happen, but ignorance is bliss, and costly!

As is always the case when a pet gains rapid popularity, it is

The author with his favorite hedgehog, one of the many that he keeps.

Entertaining, even fascinating, hedgehogs provide endless amusement.

surrounded by a great deal of misinformation. There are then those breeders who have little thought for what they are doing. They mate any individual to any other in order to produce as many offspring as they can. Often, close matings were evident, and sows bred before they were mature, thus increasing the already inbred state of the species as a domestic pet.

The effect of poor breeding policy is that temperament often suffers. This soon started to be apparent in this charming little animal.

The African hedgehog was banned from further importation during the early 1990s, this being a mixed blessing. On the one hand, it is always preferable to purchase domestically bred stock.

But on the other hand, the fact that the ban was implemented when only a relatively small population existed was the direct cause of rapid escalation in prices (as was the case with the potbellied pig). In comparison, in another rising little pet known as the sugar glider, the availability of wild imports has kept prices reasonable.

In April 1993 the North American Hedgehog Association (NAHA) was founded. This organization has, in its short history, achieved much to help stabilize the hobby and provide a guiding influence that is needed once the initial frenzy of high-priced breeding is over. The year 1994 ended with the publication of this author's first book on these pets. The book was published by T.F.H. Publications, which has always been the market leader in disseminating vital information on new pets. It was following the success of the first book that this work was commissioned, enabling more information to be recorded. It must be kept in mind that the domestic history of the hedgehog is still being made, so each new work has something to add to that which has gone before.

Within the following chapters everything you need to know about hedgehogs is detailed so that you can select and care for these pets in the correct manner. The magnificent photography, much of it by Ralph Lermayer, himself a NAHA judge, co-founder and first president of that association, brings the essence of these pets into your home. The work is the embodiment not only of my

In the wild, hedgehogs spend a lot of time foraging for food. They are very methodical as they go about this activity.

TFH has committed itself to a number of works on this pet so that hobbyists will have access to progressively more information as it is made available. Such a policy is always of immeasurable value in helping to stabilize a new pet and ensures that owners have up-to-the minute advice via books.

own experiences as a breeder, but also of those of many leading founder breeders across this country who have contributed information to me when it was needed. To these dedicated people I am indebted.

Having briefly detailed the hobby to date, let us now focus on

The hedgehog's ability to roll itself into a ball for protection is one of its special traits.

the hedgehog to see just why it has proven to be such a tremendously popular pet. What indeed makes for the ideal pet? This, of course, is a subjective question because the perfect pet will probably never exist.

First and foremost, the hedgehog is a challenging pet, the likes of which have never been seen before in small mammal form. It is very unforgiving of mistreatment and poor breeding. Its evolutionary defensive strategy of curling into a ball of prickly spines means that if it is not treated kindly, it will hardly be the perfect companion.

Conversely, treat it gently, and it will delight you by laying down its spines like a stiff brush. It will happily sit on your lap or shoulder, or it will busy itself by exploring your home. It has no natural odor you can detect (assuming it is housed in clean quarters) and is neither noisy nor destructive in comparison to such pets as dogs, cats, or even rabbits.

Hedgehogs are often given complete freedom to roam their owners' homes. They will get along just fine with most other house pets, like dogs and cats, whom they will largely ignore, and who will ignore them once their

Hedgehogs know that areas that are protected from sunlight are good places to find various insects, which are a staple of their diet.

Hedgehogs will also eagerly explore woodpiles in their efforts to find suitable foods.

novelty has worn off. These pets are very easy to feed, and their upkeep cost is remarkably low.

Hedgehogs are not at all difficult to breed if provided with the correct conditions. They are fastidiously clean and in many ways extremely hardy. Although not especially long-lived, they can be expected to achieve five to seven years under good conditions.

No pet is all things to all people, the hedgehog being no exception to this rule. It is not a cuddly pet suited to small children not yet at the age of understanding, nor is it suited to those who want one just to be "in fashion." You should not purchase any pet without much prior thought. But if you are the sort of person who appreciates a pet that is a little different and responds to care and attention, then it is very probable you will be well suited to this small insectivore.

This mother hedgehog is teaching her youngsters how to forage. This activity usually begins when the youngsters are about five weeks of age.

Natural History

One of the very sad things to be said about many pet owners is that they go out and purchase pets without first learning something about them as living creatures. Were they to take just a little time to obtain such information, they might possibly avoid the situation whereby they own a pet and then find they are ill equipped to care for its needs. This is especially true where the "exotic" species are concerned.

If you have a basic understanding of what a hedgehog is all about in its wild state, you start with a very sound platform of knowledge on its likely needs and reactions in captivity. It is therefore appropriate that we look at the hedgehog from a natural history standpoint. Many books have been written on hedgehogs over the years, most being centered on the European species. In this chapter, no attempt will be made to delve too deeply into the subject, it being more of a primer that will give you basic information on the pet you have purchased or are about to purchase.

THE WAY ANIMALS ARE CLASSIFIED

There are over one million species of animals on our planet. In order to refer to them in some sort of meaningful manner, zoologists divide them into a series of mutually similar groups. These groups are then divided into further groups, the process being repeated until one arrives at the one million or so species men-

As this photo clearly shows, Atelerix albiventris *was named for its white belly.*

Camouflage is one of the hedgehog's most effective defenses against natural predators.

tioned. At the peak of what may be compared to a pyramid is the all-embracing group (kingdom) known as Animalia—the animals (as compared to bacteria or plants).

This group commences with the most simple life forms. From it, the groups below become more and more complex in their features. We need not consider the higher ranks of formal classification because they are differentiated by such things as whether they house single- or multi-celled organisms, whether they have a central notochord, or not, and so on. Our interest starts at what is called the class rank. Here we see such groups as Insecta (insects), Reptilia (reptiles), Aves (birds) and Osteichthyes (bony fish). Each of these groups (and many more) are defined as such by a number of features their members collectively share. This may be in possessing scales, feathers, gills, simple or complex blood circulations, or in methods of reproduction and other characteristics. Rarely does a group display a single diagnostic feature, it being defined by the possession of numerous features. Another, and very important, class of animals is that called Mammalia, the mammals. We are members of this class, as are dogs, cats, mice, elephants, whales—and hedgehogs. The similarities that all members display are that they have hair, are warm blooded, breath via lungs, have a complex blood circulatory system, are placental in their method of reproduction, and the females suckle their offspring on milk via modified sweat glands—teats.

There are about 4,500 mammalian species, which are divided into a series of groups. This major group level (rank) is known as ordinal, each being called an order. There are 21 mammalian orders, the most populous in respect of members being Rodentia, the rodents, which contains no less than 1,814 species. The second largest group is Chiroptera, the bats. This contains 986 species. Our interest is centered on the order that has the third largest number of species: it is called Insectivora, the insect eaters. It houses about 390 species.

are merely basic terms applied to a group of animals, and which reflect a major feature of them. This does not suggest they are by any means definitive descriptions. Dogs and cats are in the order Carnivora—the flesh eaters.

But humans eat flesh too, as do whales, rodents, hedgehogs and many other animals. These are carnivorous species without being members of that order of animals, which is restricted to dogs, cats, weasels, bears and their like (all of which also eat insects).

The order Insectivora is, in the view of some scientists, a very

The hedgehog is a member of the mammalian order known as Insectivora, which also includes moles, shrews, and tenrecs. All of these animals have pointed noses that enable them to scent out insects and other livefoods.

INSECTIVORES

The first thing you must not do when learning a major group name, such as Insectivora, is to take it too literally. Ordinal, and many other rank or group names,

poorly defined group of animals. In some ways it may be regarded as a catch-all type group in which zoologists have dumped a number of species because there seemed no better place to put

This is a perfect example of self-anointing, one of the hedgehog's most baffling habits.

them. This said, the members do share a range of features.

These are very primitive animals, being regarded as the earliest type of placental (eutherian) mammals. This means animals that retain their offspring internally, and which are nourished by their mother via a placenta.

eyes, up to 44 teeth (one of the largest numbers in any group of mammals), five toes on each foot, and an outer covering that can be fur, or a combination of spines and fur. Clavicles are present in all species except those of one genera, of which there are 65 housed in 7 families within the order.

Hedgehogs evolved spines as a means of defense.

From an evolutionary viewpoint, the insectivores trace their origins back over 100 million years ago (mid Cretaceous) when the dinosaurs were very much the ruling life forms. From these early insectivores, other extant (present) mammalian orders are thought to have developed.

Members of the order include the gymnures, hedgehogs, solenodons, tenrecs, moles, and shrews (excluding the elephant shrews).

Features of the order include long snouts, relatively small to no

Insectivores are nearly all nocturnal in their habits. They are found in Europe, Asia, America, Africa, Indonesia, and most other large land masses and islands, but are not native to Antarctica, Australia, New Zealand, the West Indies or the Arctic islands. Some species, such as the hedgehog, were introduced to New Zealand, possibly elsewhere, by early European settlers, while the tenrec has been introduced to some Indian Ocean islands.

THE FAMILY ERINACEIDAE—THE HEDGEHOGS

The term "hedgehog" has no scientific meaning but is a common name normally applied to the spiny-coated members of the family Erinaceidae, one of the seven families that comprise the order Insectivora. It is also used to describe certain members of the family Tenrecidae—the tenrecs.

Erinaceidae may be conveniently divided into two subfamilies, these being Galericinae (=Echinosoricinae), the gymnures or moonrats, and Erinaceinae, the hedgehogs (Corbet, 1988). We are concerned here only with the hedgehogs. But it can be mentioned that gymnures are small rodent-like mammals that have no spines, even though they are close relatives of the hedgehogs.

There are, depending on the classification you are following, about fourteen species of hedgehogs, together with a variable number of subspecies. They are placed into four genera: *Erinaceus, Atelerix, Paraechinus, and Hemiechinus.* Distribution is Europe and Asia to China, and throughout Africa.

The family is thought to have evolved in North America during the late Palaeocene period (60 million years ago), and spread to Asia during the Eocene period (54 million years ago). During the same period, it spread to Europe, and finally to Africa in the Miocene period, about 20 million years ago.

Because of their small size—about the size of a guinea pig—hedgehogs can easily get into various nooks and crannies.

DESCRIPTION

Size: Hedgehogs range in head and body size from 14-31cm (5.5-

12 in.), with the tails being 1-4cm (0.4-1.6 in.). The genus *Erinaceus* exhibits the largest size range, *Atelerix* the smallest, based on upper size potential. However, size alone is not a useful identification guide because the smaller individuals of *Atelerix* will normally be larger than their counterparts in the other three genera. In other words, the sizes within all species are such that they overlap in all but their extremes.

Weight: At 1,100g (39 oz.), possibly more, *Erinaceus* spp is potentially the heaviest, with *Atelerix* spp being the lightest at 236g (8 oz.) at the low end of its range. Once again, do not read too much into distinction of species via their weight. The overlap in range across all species is comparable. You must also bear in mind that the upper limit seen in *Erinaceus* is probably for an individual at peak weight just before hibernation. The season of the year, therefore, has considerable influence on weight, especially in the species that enter full hibernation.

Conformation: Hedgehogs are stocky little critters whose legs look rather small and weak for the body size they support. Yet those legs are surprisingly powerful. The front ones are strong enough to take the entire weight of the animal when it wants to haul itself onto a rock or similar obstacle.

The snout is elongate and pointed, the upper jaw appearing to extend over the lower, though this is, in fact, the nasal area rather than the jaw actually being any longer. The eyes are round and of medium size, appearing neither too large nor small. The erect ears range from small to large, depending on the species.

The spines cover the crown of the head, the back, and the sides of the body.

Even though a hedgehog's legs are short, they are strong enough to enable the hedgehog to climb up onto logs and rocks.

The tail is short and sparsely furred. The fur on the face, chest and underparts is soft, ranging from very silky to more coarse, depending on the individual. There are five digits on each foot, although in *Atelerix* the hallux (big toe) of the hind feet may be missing or rudimentary, thus the common name of four-toed. The digits are armed with sharp claws, which help in their fossorial (adapted for digging) lifestyle. The typical dental formula is 36 teeth, though this can vary.

Spines: The head, back and flanks are covered with spines that range in size to over 2.5cm (1 in.), depending on the species. These spines are smooth and non-barbed in all species other than those of *Paraechinus*, whose spines display a slight wavy (rugose) surface.

On the head of three of the genera there is a quite distinct spineless tract that runs medially, and which is lacking in *Hemiechinus*. This tract, or channel, is very obvious to see in newly born individuals, running the entire length of the body. In adults, it is seen only on the head. Its width is about 2mm in *Atelerix*, slightly less in *Erinaceus*, and somewhat more in *Paraechinus*. When the mantle spines are laid flat against the crown, it is most readily noticed.

The spines of hedgehogs do not cause birth problems for the mother because they are very soft and covered in a sheath. I am told that the initial spines are shed and replaced as the youngster grows. If this is the case, it is over an extended period of time because there is no evidence at all of heavy shedding in *Atelerix* under captive conditions.

In adults, the spines appear to be shed only when the individual is either ill or stressed. However, whether or not there is a slow but steady shedding of spines throughout the hedgehog's life does not appear to have been well documented.

It is difficult to determine this under captive conditions due to the substrate of shavings that are most commonly used, and which would mask limited numbers of spines. The spines are not released as a protective measure as are those of a porcupine's tail.

The hedgehog can alter the angle at which the spines are pointed in order to achieve maximum defense. Under normal conditions, the spines lay flat to the body. They become partially raised when danger threatens and can be directed at an angle of over 45 degrees when danger is imminent, becoming criss-crossed on the body at maximum defensive posture.

Sexual Differences: The only way the sexes are determined is

When it is on the ground, a hedgehog is capable of picking up scents below the surface to a depth of about an inch or more.

In sharp contrast with the spines, the fur on the face, chest, and belly is quite soft.

by inspection of their underparts. In the male, the penis is sheathed, partly pendulous, pointed forward, and located approximately where you would expect the navel to be—abdominally. In the female, the anus and vagina are close together. Sexes can be ascertained almost from birth, the only potential error likely to be in mistaking the umbilical cord for a penis in males only a few days old. The number of mammae is variable, but normally up to five pairs, depending on species.

Color: This is very variable, ranging from albino (red-eyed white) to melanistic (almost black). Most individuals, however, will sport spines displaying an agouti pattern, which is created by horizontal bands of white, brown and cream. This color pattern is named for the South American rodent. The extent of melanin within the spinal shaft will influence the perceived color. Under domestic conditions, a number of color variants have been established.

The soft fur on a hedgehog also ranges in color, from white to light and dark brown, to almost black. The face may carry a mask of varying color intensity, the colors being even or blotchy. All species sport sensitive vibrissae (whiskers).

Sensory abilities: The eyesight of hedgehogs is probably good by insectivoral standards, but it can be regarded only as adequate for its needs rather than good by our standards, and that of other diurnal animals (those active during daylight hours).

Wild hedgehogs spend the hot hours of the day in cool shelter and emerge to feed and roam during the cool of the morning and evening.

Hedgehogs are solitary animals and come together only to mate.

Its keenest senses are undoubtedly smell and hearing—in that order. It is able to pick up high frequency sounds, such as those of insects. Having located the direction, it will proceed toward it until within scenting range. It can pick up scents much as a dog can: by lifting its nose into the air and sniffing.

At ground level, it is able to scent beneath the surface to about an inch or more and will then use its claws to dig down for the snack hiding below the soil. It cannot be regarded as an especially intelligent creature, which is not to say it displays no intelligence.

VOCALIZATIONS

Hedgehogs are capable of making a number of sounds, some very audible, others much less so.

The most significant are the following.

Aggression: This sound is like a rapidly repeated te-te-te, as in terrain. It is accompanied by head butting. A softer hissing-clicking kind of noise is made when the hedgehog is curled in a ball and feels threatened.

Apprehension: This is a muted vibration; a rolled constant sound.

Birthing: The only familiar sound I can relate this to is the cooing of a dove. It is a short sound emitted by the mother at the moment of birth.

Pain: You will have no problems identifying this sound, and I hope you never have to react to it. It ranges from a very high-pitched screech to a much softer, but very sad, sound after the initial screech.

The hedgehog's keenest senses are those of smell and hearing—in that order.

Contentment/interest: This is a very quiet intermittent sound made when hedgehogs are foraging.

It should be pointed out that newly born hedgehogs squeal sporadically when they want the attention of their mother. This can prompt the owner to think something is amiss (which, of course, might be the case), but usually there is no problem.

HABITATS

Hedgehogs live in a wide variety of habitats determined by the environment to which they are native. At one extreme, they may be adapted to live in arid desert regions, at the other in the lush conditions of lightly timbered deciduous forests and grasslands. They prefer to live where there are low bushes or craggy rocks in which they can take refuge. Wetlands are avoided, as are heavily wooded coniferous forests.

During the warmer months, hedgehogs will satisfy their home needs simply by burrowing under a pile of leaves, or curl into a ball beneath bushes. They are quite happy to venture into human settlements, where they will take up residence under sheds, buildings, log piles, and their like.

Indeed, in most countries, distinction should be made between the urban and country hedgehogs. This affects many facets of their lives. The two types do not readily adapt to living in that which is alien to them, for example, if perchance they should be transplanted after receiving treatment for injury for example.

With the onset of colder weather, and when breeding, hedgehogs will seek out a more secure den. This will be either a shallow burrow that they will dig themselves, or a burrow taken over or left by a previous non-hedgehog resident.

LIFESTYLE

All hedgehogs are basically nocturnal, though they may on occasion become crepuscular (active at dawn and dusk) when the need arises. They are better able than many other nocturnal animals to cope with daylight but will always try to avoid bright direct sunlight.

Hedgehogs are very active little animals well able to move at a quite goodly speed when the need arises. They are capable climbers, though when coming down from heights they are best compared to cats—ungainly! Although water is a commodity used only for drinking, they can swim—again, if the need arises.

Hedgehogs follow well-defined pathways during their food-foraging expeditions. These pathways are developed over a period of time, starting from when they first accompany their mother on short trips. The older they get, the wider the circle of their range, which extends until it is satisfactory to meet their nutritional needs.

Diet: Hedgehogs are very cosmopolitan in their tastes, which span a considerable range of items. Chief among these are invertebrates—insects and their larvae, such as mealworms, worms of various species, caterpillars, crickets, slugs, snails, centipedes, aphids (greenfly), and their like. Not all beetles or in-

This hedgehog is allowed free roam of a secure yard and garden, helping to keep these tomato plants naturally bug free.

sects are eaten because some release odors that hedgehogs obviously find offensive.

Hedgehogs will also eat any small creatures they come across at ground level, such as frogs, baby mice, lizards, snakes, fallen nestling birds and eggs, spiders, even small scorpions in the case of the desert hedgehogs. They will also eat carrion. Urban hedgehogs are frequent visitors to trash dumps, where they will forage for household scraps.

A wild hedgehog may eat a daily quantity of food equal to one third of its weight. Most of this is needed to sustain its very active lifestyle, and the tissues worn out as a result of this. Under restricted captive conditions, this level of food intake would result in obesity. Also, in wild hedgehogs of northern climates, considerable weight gain must be made during the warmer months to prepare for hibernation.

However, stories of their chasing and attacking adult mice, or any creature that is healthy and lively, are overly exaggerated. The hedgehog can normally find sufficient foods on its foraging trips so that it doesn't have a need to tackle any but the very smallest of prey, or prey that is unable to defend itself.

Whether or not "pack" attacking is a feature of these animals seems not to have been documented. However, personal observation of both sexes "attacking" a leather glove in numbers would suggest that a female and offspring old enough to travel with her are capable of this.

Although these insectivores will eat some fruit and vegetable

This hedgehog has stopped to consume a small edible as it goes about its morning forage.

Color varies in hedgehogs, ranging from white to almost black; but most of them display agouti coloration on the spines: bands of white, brown, and cream.

matter, the amount is very limited. Fruits that are eaten will likely be those that have fallen from trees and are probably overly ripe. Additionally, they probably contain the larvae of some insect or other. The same is no doubt true of vegetables and nuts, both of which may be taken when the hedgehog is really hungry. Hedgehogs are generally welcome both by householders and farmers because they do no damage to crops or plants; indeed, they will consume many of the insects that damage crops and plants. At the same time, any nestling mice that are taken is regarded as a bonus.

Social Life: Hedgehogs are essentially solitary animals, the two sexes coming together merely to perpetuate the species. The female alone rears the young, which she weans when they are four to six weeks of age. Thereafter, they will remain with the mother for possibly a few more weeks before eventually wandering off to find their own territory. Males are very aggressive to each other during courtship fights for a female.

Hibernation: Hedgehogs living in the northern countries of their range will enter periods of hibernation when the ambient temperature drops below a certain level.

Estivation: In the hotter countries, such as Africa, hedgehogs estivate rather than hibernate. This means they will become torpid and enter a light sleep when either the weather gets too hot or food is in short supply.

The interesting thing about these two dormant states is that they are seen at opposite ends of the temperature range. This suggests that they have internal mechanisms that dramatically slow down metabolism in response to both cold *and* heat. Further, the availability of food may also influence this state as much during cold weather as when it is hot. The two may be intrinsically linked.

lizards. In the case of the larger predators having long claws, they are able to strike repeated blows at the motionless ball of prickles and in this way kill it. Rats have been known to eat away at the spines until they can attack a soft part—but of course may themselves be badly injured in the

An old flowerpot serves as a suitable retreat for this hedgehog.

PREDATORS

The hedgehog's very prickly defense system provides a good deterrent against most potential aggressors, but even so a number are able to overcome this and prey on the animal. Included among these are bears, wild dogs, wolves, foxes, badgers, eagles, owls, and even rats. There can be little doubt that the list is more extensive than this and probably includes weasels, martens, even the larger cats, as well as very large

process. Large birds of prey are able to withstand the spines with their powerful beaks and talons. Snakes, even poisonous species, will generally leave the hedgehog well alone. When attempts to strike at it are made, the result is invariably damage to the snake's face. Indeed, unless it is very careful, the smaller snake may end up being killed by the hedgehog. This will be achieved by a bite into its back or neck then hanging on while half curling its body to protect it from being bitten. Hedgehogs are not immune to snake poison as some people believe, but they are able to withstand amounts that would easily kill other animals of their own size and larger.

manner—each suddenly trying a burst of pushing. Once they grasp soft underskin or a rear leg, they will shake it violently, hanging on as long as they can before the opponent is able to free itself.

In the author's experience,

A moonlight swim...

FIGHTING

When hedgehogs fight, they will do so by trying to overturn their opponent in order to grasp hold of the soft underparts. They approach to the side and then turn their heads to the middle of the opponent. In turn, the defender will lean its body over toward the attacker—sometimes to such a degree that it can topple over, but it will then quickly form a tight impenetrable ball. At other times, attacks are targeted at the rear flank of the opponent, these usually being the more successful. The antagonists will turn many circles in a head to rear end

females rarely fight, so they can be housed together without problems in captivity if given sufficient space.

Males, however, are far more tenacious toward each other when they do fight, so they are best kept as singles in captivity. This having been said, the author has maintained males in good harmony under ecosystem (habitat) conditions once they really got to know each other.

There is definitely a compatibility factor involved where males are concerned, and in the majority of cases they are not compatible! The slightest changes in their

In areas in which they are indigenous, hedgehogs are welcomed by farmers and gardeners because they help to control the insect population.

home habitat may prompt them to become belligerent toward each other. These comments are based on *Atelerix* species. It may be that members of this species are somewhat more social than those of other genera. This is difficult to determine, as there are only scattered reports on the captive social status of species in other genera.

The water's edge usually offers an abundance of insects.

The Hedgehog Species

It is not essential to have any particular knowledge of the hedgehog species, or of how they are classified, when keeping one as a pet. However, many owners like to understand the basics of the subject from an interest viewpoint. Certainly, without appreciating the grass roots of natural history and nomenclature, you could not be termed a serious enthusiast.

Unfortunately, this practice is evident in other pets, such as in Amazonian and other parrots, within numerous popular tropical fish, and in the potbellied pig, to cite but three examples.

The consequence is that these animals are sold as being a given species (or variety) when they are actually hybrids. The problem that subsequently arises is that if their offspring are advertised as

Hedgehogs will carefully sniff any objects that are foreign to them.

THE PROBLEMS OF HYBRIDIZATION

For breeders, an understanding of how species are created is fundamental to their knowledge. Without this knowledge, they are more likely to hybridize their animals, which has no merit to a true hobbyist.

being of a given species, a serious breeder might obtain one. That person would very disappointed to find a hybrid had been purchased, with the attendant problems created when trying to get his cash back.

Alternatively, the person may begin using the hybrid in a breeding program, unaware that it is not the species he thought it was. This hybrid aspect of a pet species is worthy of some comment here because it is already happening with hedgehogs. You should therefore know how it comes about.

It has to be said that when species are very similar in appearance, as is the case in hedgehogs, it can indeed be all but impossible to determine the species unless its original source was documented, and its onward breeding carefully monitored and recorded. This was certainly not the case in hedgehogs now popular as pets in the USA.

This comment is based on the author's research via personal communication with the early breeders into the source of stock used in the present breeding lines, from which most American hedgehogs have been produced. I have photographs of tenrecs that were sold as African pygmy hedgehogs, which really underscores the problem.

Fortunately, the limited initial pool of stock in the USA appears to have been of the genus *Atelerix*, so most hedgehogs will be of that genus. The present danger, and the reason for this discussion, is that there are other species in the USA. There is little doubt that some hedgehogs have been illegally imported into the country. This compounds matters.

If desert hedgehogs are hybridized with the African pygmy (assuming they will indeed hybridize to produce fertile offspring), they will introduce their genes to both members of a paired species. Subsequently, these may sud-

Hedgehogs can be found in Europe, Africa, and Asia. They were introduced by humans into New Zealand.

This hedgehog is about ready to go to sleep. In the wild, hedgehogs are most active between the hours of dusk and dawn.

denly turn up in what was thought to be "pure" African pygmy stock and prompt the owner to think a new mutation has appeared in the species. Once this happens, it really can create many problems, so it is best to try to avoid the situation in the first place, which is only possible if you know something about the species. It then requires the existence of a breeding register, which is what the North American Hedgehog Association is currently creating, including those for other than the most popular species.

WHAT IS A SPECIES?

If species have overlapping distributions, they are said to be sympatric. If they are separated geographically, they are allopatric. A sibling species is a "good" species in that it retains its species status by not hybridizing with other closely related species, even though their distributions overlap. Yet on purely morphological grounds, it is not readily distinguishable from certain other species.

It may, however, display numerous other features, such as its gestation period, number of offspring, social habits, or even feeding habits, that make it a good species.

A subspecies is any group of animals that are clearly of a given species but that, due to a physical barrier, such as a lake, river, or mountain range, have become separated from their root stock. They show consistent minor differences from them. They may not always be separated from their root stock but have already begun the process of speciation by

When foraging, hedgehogs waddle along at a leisurely pace; but they are capable of surprisingly quick bursts of speed.

displaying consistent differences to their root stock.

With the passage of time, subspecies may become so different from their original root stock that they will become full species. By this means, evolution proceeds. But this generally only happens in the larger life forms, such as hedgehogs, over periods of time that are counted in hundreds of years, even millenniums.

Only by studying many hundreds, indeed thousands, of individuals can a zoologist separate these various forms into logical species, subspecies, and sibling species groups. However, this is not always done because of the time, effort, and costs involved. Scientists anxious to be credited for naming a new species will label it as such on what may later prove to be quite unacceptable grounds.

Below the level of subspecies, but not recognized by zoologists in formal classifications, are variants or sports. All animals display very minor differences that make them individuals, no two individuals ever being carbon copies—not even twins.

Variants can arise from mutation, from malfunction of cells, from prenatal illness, and similar metabolic disturbances. In all but those based on mutation, their morphological variation will not be passed on to their offspring. Even mutations that display striking changes, especially of color, are unlikely to survive in the wild, unless it offers them an advantage over the normal colors, which is rarely the case.

THE HEDGEHOG SPECIES

From the foregoing discussion, you can appreciate that once you move from very obvious morphologically different species of hedgehogs, it becomes very debatable where to draw lines on what is and is not a species. This is especially so when it comes to subspecies. Subspecies may be only reasonably established by examination of cranial bones, dentition and other internal parts, and even these give rise to disagreement—which is why you need, at the least, hundreds of examples for comparison and study. Classifications may vary among different books: one authority may not agree with another over the standing of given regional forms. Some authorities will tend to keep things as simple as possible—they are called lumpers. Others seem determined to divide genus members into as many species and subspecies as they can on the flimsiest of evidence—they are known as splitters. Who is correct? Only by long-term studies can you make an assessment. Until then, you follow a given authority for whatever reasons you feel are valid. Usually, because it is their classification you have read—hardly a scientific basis, but it's a start!

Armed with the information that you gain, you will be more cautious in the mating of hedgehogs that clearly differ from each other, based on the descriptions that follow shortly.

SCIENTIFIC NOMENCLATURE

The present system of naming animals is called the binomial system of nomenclature. It is based on the works of Swedish naturalist Carolus Linnaeus

Many people think that hedgehogs are related to porcupines because they have spines, but this isn't so: hedgehogs are insectivores, and porcupines are rodents. The two species simply happened to evolve a similar means of defense.

(1707-1778), specifically that of the tenth edition of his *Systema Naturae,* 1758. Unlike his earlier editions, where polynomials were used to name animals, in the edition stated he used just two names. They are the genera (singular, genus) and the trivial or specific. The genus is the major rank below that of family; the species is the major rank below genus. At the rank of family, the members are very similar in many of their features. They become even more so at subfamily rank, and yet more so again at genus level.

Within a genus are found clearly identifiable groups of individuals that can be distinguished from the "type" that defines the genus. By being given their own unique name within that genus, they are thus identified. Because the same trivial or specific names can be used in other genera, it is only when they are combined with the generic name that a species is uniquely identified. A specific name can be used but once in any given genus of animals. Thus, *europaeus* is not the species name of the European hedgehog, but *Erinaceus europaeus* is.

The genus is normally printed in a typeface that differs from the main text, usually appearing in italics. The same is true of the species and subspecies. Ranks above the genus appear in normal typeface. When a subspecies is recognized, the procedure is as follows. The original type on which the species was named has its trivial name repeated, forming a trinomial. The subspecies then has its own trinomial trivial. For example, the Western European hedgehog has the species name of *Erinaceus europaeus.* To distinguish it from the Spanish hedgehog, the western race became what is called the nominate race, or form: it is *Erinaceus europaeus europaeus.* The Spanish race became *Erinacaeus europaeus hispanicus.* You can thus always establish the original type on which a species was named because of its repeated trivial name.

COMMON NAMES

Although the average hobbyist will come to know a given animal by its common name, he should also be familiar with its scientific name. Only this has any realistic value in scientific circles. The scientific name is totally international in its application. It does not change when used, or written, in other languages. This means there can be no error in the species under discussion.

There are no regulations controlling the use of a common name. It is entirely possible for a species to have many common names. Each language will use names in that language, and a species may be known by different names in different localities. Clearly, this means these names are of very limited value and can, and do, create considerable confusion.

Sometimes, through convention of use, one of the common names will become closely associated with a given species, as is the case with the African pygmy hedgehog: even so, this is still an unreliable means of identification. The scientific name should always be given in articles, books, lectures, educational bulletins, and so forth, that are intended for serious enthusiasts.

THE SPECIES

In the following section, the fourteen species of hedgehogs are described, commencing with those of the genus *Atelerix*, which is the one housing the popular pet that has created such an interest in this group of animals. It was not considered necessary to discuss subspecies in this work because of their more debatable status, and limitations of space. The listing follows that of Walker (1991), which was based on Corbet (1988).

Genus *Atelerix*

Pomel, 1848; African pygmy hedgehogs. There are four species in this genus, which is regarded by some authorities as being a subgenus of *Erinaceus*. Others have suggested that *A. frontalis* and *A. algirus* should be in their own genus of *Aethechinus*.

Atelerix albiventris. A. Albiventris has the common names of African pygmy, East African, dwarf, white-bellied, or four-toed hedgehog. The first name just listed is the one gaining most acceptance, though possibly not being the most appropriate, given that *albiventris* means white-bellied in Latin.

Distribution: From Senegal on the coast of West Africa, east to Sudan and Kenya, and south to Zambia in Southern Africa. It is thus equatorial, the Tropics of Cancer (north) and Capricorn (south) being just beyond its range.

Habitat: Mainly savanna and scrub; common around parks, gardens, and refuse sites.

Body: Length of head and body averages 16.5-23.5cm (6.5-9.2 in.); tail, 17.50mm (0.7-1.9 in.). Weight range is 236-700g (8-25 oz.). The typical weight range within domestic forms is 312-454g (11-16 oz).

The color of the face and feet ranges from light to dark brown. The feet often display gray, either solid or mottled. Walker (1991) states that the underparts range from white to black, but white-cream is predominant in domestic forms. Spine color is regionally variable, being determined by the width of the melanin band in each spine.

The species is sexually active year 'round in its wild habitat, but the main breeding season will be October-March, which corresponds to the warm and wet seasons when plants (thus insects) are especially plentiful.

A colony of three adults and four juveniles from Togo, possibly the first controlled breeding program in the USA, was established at Adelphi University, New York, in 1976. These were classified as *A. pruneri*, which is not treated at species rank in this text. The essential results were documented by Brodie (1982).

The interesting aspect of that program was that while imported wild examples were bred (11 of 28 litters were raised), success with captive-bred stock was quite the opposite. Only 1 of 31 litters produced from domestically bred females were raised to maturity. Other aspects of the program illustrate just how far *albiventris* has come over the years in its captive breeding record. The article is well worth obtaining.

The tendency of domestic-bred females to reject their offspring was very apparent in the program. The conclusion this author draws from comparisons with the present situation is that changes in the rate at which the endocrine glands secrete adrenalin have taken place. This reduces the nervous state of females.

Atelerix frontalis. South African, or white-browed hedgehog. Much of that applying to *albiventris* holds true for *frontalis*, whose name in Latin pertains to the forehead. The species is said to be, on average, somewhat smaller than *albiventris.*

Distribution: This is more restricted than *albiventris*. S.W. Angola to W. Zambia, Malawi and Mozambique. South through Botswana and Zimbabwe to South Africa.

Whereas *albiventris* estivates, this species may be said to hibernate during the colder periods (May-August) of its more southerly ranges, emerging from the estivation if the weather suddenly gets warmer.

As a result of its popularity, both as a pet and as a food delicacy, *frontalis* was said to be scarce by Meester as far back as 1975 and was officially placed on the list of rare and threatened species (CITES 2) in 1985. As a consequence, you are unlikely to see this species in the USA.

Atelerix sclateri. Sclater's, Somali, or East African hedgehog. Sclater's hedgehog is described as being very similar to *albiventris*, but with brown underparts and five toes on the rear feet. Its distribution appears to be restricted to northern Somalia (Walker, 1991). If this is true, which seems unlikely, it has the smallest distribution of any of the African species. Its range is allopatric to that of others in the genus, but sympatric with that of *Paraechinus aethiopicus.*

Atelerix algirus. Algerian, or wandering, hedgehog. The Algerian, or wandering, hedgehog (the latter being named for the species *A. vagans* by some authorities), is said to walk higher on the leg than others of the genus, and to have somewhat large ears. Its soft fur ranges in color from white to brown.

It is distributed from Morocco on the west coast of Africa, east through Algeria to Libya. It is also found on the Canary and Balaeric Islands, as well as in Spain, and as far north as southern France. It is thought that it may have been introduced to these islands, as well as to Europe.

The gestation period is reported as 35-48 days, rather longer than others in the genus, but in most other features it appears to be typical of *Atelerix* members.

A trusting, well-bred hedgehog will allow you to examine it closely. Jagged ear tips may indicate that the animal is older or may simply be a case of siblings' chewing on the only readily accessible part of the hedgehog's anatomy.

Genus *Paraechinus*

There are three members in the genus, one being native to North Africa, one from the Middle East, and one from Asia. Although the ears are described as being small, they appear, from photographic evidence, to be slightly larger than *Atelerix* but smaller than *Hemiechinus* — possibly an adaptation for increased heat radiation, as well as for more accurate sound distinction.

The spines of *P. aethiopicus* appear to be somewhat longer than those of *Atelerix* species, but whether or not this is true for others of the genus I cannot say, as I have not seen examples of them.

The size range is 14-27cm (5.5-10.6 in.), weight being 312-435g (11-15 oz.). Litter size in the genus is one to six, the average being species dependent. Coloration is extremely variable, ranging from almost white to almost black, the soft furred parts reflecting the all-over spine colors (being either light or dark).

The spineless tract on the forehead is the widest seen in hedgehogs, but it is variable enough that it cannot be regarded as a diagnostic feature. However, the wavy spines are diagnostic of the genus.

P. aethiopicus. Distributed in Mauritania and Morocco on the west coast of Africa, east through Algeria, Libya, Egypt, and the Sudan to northern Somalia. Thence east to Arabia and Iran. The species is sympatric with each of the other genera in some parts of its distribution.

P. hypomelas. Based on a translation of its Greek name, which means black underneath, it must be assumed that this species is typical of the darker forms of the genus. Also known as Brandt's hedgehog, it is native from the Aral Sea, southeast to Pakistan and northern India, and southwest to southern Iran and the southern Arabian peninsula.

P. micropus. We can assume from its name that micropus, meaning small-footed in Greek, is the smallest of this genus. Its litter numbers of one to two would further support this view. It is native to Pakistan, western and southern India.

Genus *Hemiechinus*

Fitzinger, 1866. Long-eared desert hedgehogs. The most aberrant hedgehog genus, it houses four species. Features of these animals are the long ears that rise above the head spines, the long legs, and the lack of a median spineless tract.

Length is in the range of 15-28cm (5.9-11 in.), the weight range being 240 to over 500g (8.5-18 oz.). The gestation period is said to be 35-42 days, with a litter range of one to six, this being species variable according to altitude. Longevity is about the same as that for *albiventris*: seven years.

Although the genus members, along with those of *Paraechinus*, are commonly called desert hedgehogs, this is perhaps a little misleading to most people in that they are found in sub-desert and scrub terrain, as well as near human settlements.

Depending on your view of beauty, they are either ugly or cute. They have a mixed reputation in captivity, some owners regarding them as definitely more aggressive than other genera members, others finding them not as bad as their reputation. The latter, it must be said in fairness, is based on only a relative handful of individuals, with little comparison with most other species.

H. auritus is found in Eastern Ukraine and Mongolia, south to Libya and western Pakistan. Possibly introduced to the island of Cyprus.

H. collaris, the collared hedgehog, is native to Pakistan and northwest India.

H. dauuricus is found in the Gobi desert region to northern China.

H. hughi, Hugh's hedgehog, is found in Central China.

Genus *Erinaceus*

With a range that is more extensive than that of any other genus, it is hardly surprising that some authorities divide this one into a number of species. Here, we accept only three. The Eurasian hedgehogs have been subject to far more studies than any other genus, this being especially true of those from Western Europe.

The size range is 13.5-31cm (5.3-12 in.). Weight ranges from 400-1,100g (14-39 oz.), so the largest hedgehogs are within this genus. Gestation period is 30-40 days, litter range, is 1-8, 4 being typical. Longevity is about seven years, but it is thought that this could reach ten years under optimum conditions.

Unlike the year-round breeding ability of African species, the Eurasian hedgehogs normally have two breeding periods between May and October, thus producing only two litters per year.

In the northern parts of their range, the species will hibernate throughout the colder months, but may only estivate in the southerly regions. Differences between the Eurasian species and others is largely based on cranial features, so you will appreciate that apart from *Hemiechinus* spp, hedgehogs are essentially very similar, not displaying anything like the member differences exhibited in some mammalian families, such as cats (Felidae) or dogs (Canidae) for example.

E. europaeus. The Western European hedgehog. Found in west and central Europe, including the former Soviet Union and into Scandinavia. Indigenous to most islands including Britain, Ireland, Sicily, Sardinia, Corsica and others.

E. concolor. The name of this species means cone colored. The Eurasian hedgehog is native to eastern Europe, west Siberia, and south to Turkey, Syria, Israel, and Iraq.

E. amurensis. The Amur hedgehog. This species is native to southeast Siberia, Manchuria, Korea, and northeast China.

It is said that urban individuals

of the Western race have larger litters than their rural counterparts. This may reflect the greater feeding opportunities where humans will contribute to the menu by leaving scraps out, and by the food at the garbage dumps.

It is also said that long-snouted examples are more aggressive than are the short-muzzled individuals. However, what is more likely is that in the spring, after hibernation and with the coming breeding season, lithe examples are more active and more likely to be belligerent than in the autumn, when they are fat and beginning to become slightly torpid. In other words, snout differences are more perceived seasonally than they are in reality.

FAMILY TENRECIDAE: TENRECS

The family Tenrecidae comprises ten genera, of which four contain species that are commonly known as Madagascar hedgehogs, or spined tenrecs. Of these, two look much like other hedgehogs, the other two being more aberrant. Whether these "hedgehogs" are the product of convergent or parallel evolution I cannot say, though Brodie (1977) states that they are convergent.

This latter evolutionary path occurs when unrelated species display similar characteristics even though they are from different ancestral stock. They are evolutionary adaptations rather than being part of a phylogenetic series. Parallel evolution occurs when species of common ancestral stock, but separated over a large time span, display similar characteristics that are acquired independently due to similar ecological pressures.

The hedgehog tenrecs have interest to hedgehog owners because of their similar looks. The need to be aware of the fact that they are not true hedgehogs is underlined by the fact that examples of *Setifer setosus* have been sold as African pygmy hedgehogs (*Atelerix*).

The owners of these tenrecs will be very disappointed if they attempt to mate them with members of the true hedgehog species. Further, any disappointment in them as pets (should this be the case) will reflect negatively on the *Atelerix* species.

The hedgehog tenrecs differ from true hedgehogs in a number of characteristics. The following descriptions may enable you to distinguish between a hedgehog tenrec and a true hedgehog in cases where this is not obvious. Other information is given for interest value.

The hedgehog tenrecs are all native to Madagascar (formerly Malagasy), a large island about the size of Texas. This island lies 250 miles from the east coast of Africa. Certain tenrecs have been introduced to the nearby Comoro Islands, as well as to the Mascarene Islands (Reunion, Mauritius and Rodriguez), which lie to the east of Madagascar in the Indian Ocean, and to the Seychelles.

Genus Setifer. There is but one species, *Setifer setosus* (meaning full of bristles), with the common names of setifer or large Madagascar hedgehog. It is found in the northern parts of the island. In size, it ranges from 15-22cm (6-9 in.). The tail is short, and weight is 6-9 oz., though it may become heavier under domestic conditions. It is therefore somewhat smaller than *Atelerix*. The vibrissae (whiskers) are longer than in the pygmy hedgehog, and the rear feet have five well-developed digits, rather than four plus a reduced hallux. The number of teeth are the same as in *Atelerix*.

The body is longer than in *Atelerix,* though given some of the slimmer pygmy hedgehogs, this is not a reliable indicator of differences. There are five pairs of mammae. Color is said to be within typical hedgehog agouti range, though the examples I have seen were all a light chocolate sort of color, including the face. There is no spineless median tract on the head, an obvious difference to *Atelerix.*

The legs and feet appear to be larger than in *Atelerix,* while the face does not seem as appealing as that of the pygmy hedgehog. The gestation period is variously reported as 51-61 days, or 65-69 days, both much longer than in any hedgehog species. Litter size averages three, within a range of one to five, although I suspect that the upper limit could be larger. Longevity is recorded as over ten years, thus it is longer than in *Atelerix*. General feeding and care needs are as for other hedgehogs.

Genus *Echinops.* This genus is also monotypic, with the single species *Echinops telfairi* native to the southern regions of Madagascar. It has the common name of small Madagascar hedgehog and is shorter and lighter in weight than *Setifer*. As with *Setifer,* its coloration is variable from pale to dark. It is not as easily distinguished from hedgehogs as is the setifer, though the absence of both a tail and a cranial spineless tract would be sufficient for identification purposes. (*Hemiechinus* also lacks these features, but its long ears make it distinguishable from a true hedgehog.)

Gestation period is reported as 42-49 days. The average litter contains five to seven, within a range of one to ten. Interestingly, the eyes of the young are said to open at nine days, rather quicker than in the pygmy hedgehog. It has 32 teeth. It is said to be quite arboreal in its habits. Females are also said to co-exist under cage conditions, even when raising litters. Longevity is excellent at a recorded 13 years.

At this time, Professor Edmund D. Brodie, Jr. maintains a small study herd of this species at Utah State University.

Genus *Hemicentetes.* Mivart, 1871. Streaked tenrec. This bizarre-looking critter has the scientific name of *Hemicentetes semispinosus*—the half-, or semi-spined, tenrec but is more commonly called the streaked tenrec. It is unusual in a number of ways. It has a length of 6-7 in. (16-19cm), so it is neither very large nor heavy—weight averaging 6-8 oz. The color is a basic black background on which there are white or brown longitudinal streaks or blotches. The under-body is brown to cream-white.

The snout and skull are long and black, while the neck sports a ruff of long spines, some of which are also found on the underbelly. Compared to hedgehogs, the legs are long. This unusual hedgehog-like animal may live in much larger burrows than is typical for others. It is more social, groups of ten comprising boars, sows, and their offspring living amicably together.

The gestation period is 55-63 days. Litters range from 1 to 11; average litter size is 3 or 7, depending on the subspecies. Sexual maturity is reached as early as five weeks, the quickest period within any hedgehog genera. The longest reported lifespan is two years and seven months. Unlike most other "hedgehogs," this species does not curl into a defensive ball but instead relies on raising its very long neck spines and butting to dissuade would-be attackers.

Genus *Tenrec*. Lacépède, 1799. This genus contains the single species *Tenrec ecaudatus,* known as the common Madagascar hedgehog. This is the species that has been introduced to islands near Madagascar. Although the trivial name indicates that there is no tail, a short one is visible. Length is 10-15 in., making this the largest of the hedgehog-like animals. Weight is in the range of 3.5-5.31 lbs.

The snout and skull are long and conical. The color pattern is agouti, giving the appearance of being either gray or brown. The coat is a mixture of spines and coarse hair, the spines not being sharp and prickly as in other hedgehog-like genera. They are longest down the spinal region. The digits are 5/5.

This tenrec is potentially an extremely prolific producer, having twelve pairs of mammae and an average litter size of 12-16, with a range of 1-32! Gestation is 55-65 days.

When annoyed, this species does not curl into a ball but instead raises its spinal hairs and hisses. It is reported to enter full hibernation during the dry season. Jones (1982) gives a captive longevity of six years and four months.

If you are looking for a pet that is a little different and responds to care and attention, a hedgehog might be just the pet for you!

Selection

Never go out and purchase a hedgehog, or any other pet, on an impulse. Sadly, this is often done. It invariably results in a pet that is an amusing novelty for a while before becoming relegated to virtual imprisonment in a cage. Here it leads a sad and often unhealthy life. Alternatively, there are always those owners, few though they may be, who profess to be pet lovers but release the animal into the wild, or in parks, when they find the pet is not suited to them, or is not what they expected. Such owners are totally lacking in any form of responsibility. They are the ones who give sustenance to those who would like to see *all* pet ownership banned. Never give a hedgehog as a pet to someone unless you are very sure they want one, and never purchase these pets for your children unless *you* like the pets as well. You must be prepared to attend to its daily needs if the child gets bored with it, which may sometimes be the case.

LEGALITY OF HEDGEHOGS

The hedgehog is classified by the United States Department of Agriculture (USDA) as a non-dangerous exotic species. As such, it can be sold as a pet by a pet store, or a breeder, without the need for a USDA license. However, if you plan to breed these pets and intend to sell them to pet stores, or to those who plan to breed them, you are required to be licensed. You do not need to be licensed to breed and sell them as pets. The fact that the USDA has given the foregoing guidelines does not mean you can legally own a hedgehog in your state. This is determined by other agencies, such as the Fish and Game Department, Department of Natural Resources, and others. Apart

The seller should have his hedgehogs, as well as any other pets, housed in well-maintained facilities.

from state regulations, which are both complex and sometimes vague or difficult to interpret, there may be local ordinances to consider.

The popularity of exotic species has created governmental and state agencies with many problems over legislation. In some instances, such as Hawaii, California, and Alaska, the regulations are quite explicit—no hedgehogs and similar exotics. In other states, the agencies are not sure themselves where this pet fits, and who determines its legal status.

Not surprisingly, this both frustrates and annoys many pet owners as being a further example of bureaucracy running amuck. A book is therefore not the appropriate place to attempt to discuss state-by-state regulations. The North American Hedgehog Association (NAHA) receives a continual flow of calls regarding the legal status of these pets. It periodically publishes updates on the position, state by state, where this information is available. It is continually striving to clarify matters that are ambiguous.

You are therefore advised to contact that association, or your local fish and game department, or the USDA, if you are unsure. Further, you are advised to contact your county hall with respect to local pet ordinances to see if the hedgehog is specifically included in them, or not. Even if your state or locality does not presently allow hedgehogs to be kept as pets, you can challenge this. Maybe, through a program of education, government agencies may reevaluate their position. This has happened in a number of states. If your state specifically prohibits these pets, you are advised not to break the law. The penalties can be severe. It is better that you campaign with others for the state to review the matter. Assuming you have considered the foregoing aspects, that you really want a hedgehog, and can legally keep one, we can now look at the numerous factors involved in the selection of a hedgehog.

GENERAL COMMENTS

The hedgehog is quite happy to

This is a spacious breeding pen, with both a dust bath and bathing pool provided in addition to the nestbox.

This type of enclosure provides the breeding female with the privacy that she requires.

live on its own, though a pair or more of females will happily live together. Indeed, they will seek the company of their own kind if given the opportunity. Males with lots of space will co-exist, but the smaller the space the greater the chance they will fight and injure each other. In spite of this belligerent attitude toward their own sex, they will still sleep together in many instances—such is the complexity of their nature. However, the best advice is not to keep two males together.

A male and female should not be kept together unless breeding is the objective. Even then, they should be separated before the sow approaches birthing. When the youngsters are weaned, do not immediately place the boar back with the sow; otherwise, she will mate again.

THE QUESTION OF AGE

A hedgehog should not be taken from its mother until it is at least six weeks of age, seven to eight weeks being much better. That extra week or two really does make a big difference to juveniles: a hedgehog can develop quite a bit in a week at this tender age. It is larger, stronger, and more independent for being left with its breeder at this time, rather than being subjected to change and high stress levels if taken too early, even if it is eating independently.

WHICH SEX?

If your hedgehog is to be just a house pet, then it does not matter which sex it is. Unlike the situation with male cats, ferrets, and other small mammals, there is no scent from a whole (non-neutered) male. What is more important in the choice of a hedgehog is how well it has been bred, and how often it is handled. These two factors are far more important than any other considerations, other than its health.

COLOR AND PATTERN

At the time of this writing, the colors seen in hedgehogs are the subject of much discussion. The NAHA is preparing official descriptions of those that are acceptable as identifiable variants. Their ruling is not available at this time, so the following is a basic information guide that will help you.

What you should understand is that some breeders will invent names in the absence of official rulings. They see this as a means of giving themselves a competitive edge. New names are appended to almost any hedgehog that looks a little different from the normal. These same breeders will ask more money for such individuals. Very often what they have is no different from another breeder's example that has been given another name, and both specimens may simply be variant "sports" of the normal wild type.

All animals have the natural ability to produce what are called "sports": offspring whose appearance is markedly different from their parents and who will not perpetuate their own kind in appearance. Some may do so because they have a genetic base. Others are simply natural variations of a basic pattern. If you see an unusual description being applied to a color or pattern, and you are not sure whether to purchase the animal in question, you

These weanlings are housed in an enclosure that allows the prospective buyer to handle and observe them easily.

are advised to contact either a NAHA judge or the association itself, which can offer guidance to help you decide.

NORMAL (WILD PATTERN)

The wild-type color pattern is called agouti. It comprises spines that have a light-colored base that gradates to brown or black, with white, cream, or yellow at the tips. When the spines are laying flat, this creates the agouti pattern named for the South American rodent. The pattern is very common in many animals because it creates a camouflage against rocks, plants, and scrub. The natural agouti color ranges from light to dark. It is under breeder selective control on what is called an additive basis. By mating light-colored stock to other specimens of the same type, you will increase the number of polygenes for lightness. The reverse is true for darkness.

The color of the spines is generally related to the color of the facial mask. Light-colored animals will usually display a light mask; dark examples will exhibit a dark mask. It should, however, be noted that the mask of youngsters is darker initially but gets lighter with maturity. The soft fur of this species in the wild varies from white to brown, but in the domestic form it is invariably, as its scientific name suggests, white to cream. The ideal agouti specimen will have an *even* pattern over its entire body. Its mask may be light or dark. The mask density is related to the all-over color. However, it will be possible, for rea-

In hedgehogs, the agouti coloration can range from light to dark.

Above and Below: *To pick a hedgehog up properly, approach from the rear with both hands palm up. Use a scooping motion and lift only after the hedgehog is secure in your hands.*

sons we need not dwell on, to consistently breed light-colored hedgehogs with dark-colored masks. This will take some time yet to achieve.

BICOLORS

A bicolored individual is one that, for genetic or environmental reasons, has distinct areas (patches, streaks, or spots) of light and dark spines. This type of

A close look at this hedgehog shows a thick coat of healthy spines, with no bald spots or signs of skin problems.

pattern is variously called salt and pepper, variegated, snowflake, harlequin, polka dot, and other names. The bicolor in hedgehogs is probably more correctly called a variegated, because more than two colors are invariably involved. Such a pattern is within the natural color range of the hedgehog. However, the pattern may be the result of genetic action, based on what is called the spotting gene, which creates piebald in horses, pied in birds, the Dutch pattern in rabbits, and other color patterns seen in domestic pets.

CREAM

The cream is a very light-colored agouti in which the melanin is greatly reduced in quantity so as to appear cream. It may be a very light agouti, or it could be the result of a genuine mutation. When two similar color patterns are seen, what you must appreciate is that if one is mutational

and the other is not, then breeding one to the other will result in only normal agouti being seen in the offspring, unless the mutation is of a dominant type.

ALBINO

The albino hedgehog is a definite mutation. It has white spines, no melanin (dark) pigment in the coat, and red eyes. If the eyes are not red, then it is not a true albino, but a dark (black) or ruby-eyed white. Albinos are true breeding to their color, whereas a white may not be so.

WHITE

The true white hedgehog, if it exists, will have a pure white coat, dark eyes, and dark points (feet and mask). It may have some yellow suffusion in the coat and spines, but this may be environmental in origin rather than genetic.

CINNAMON

The cinnamon may be nothing more than a brown-colored sport, or it may be mutational. The latter would be unlikely at this time in the development of the domestic hedgehog, but one can never tell. Only detailed breeding records will establish its mode of transmission. When selecting a hedgehog, you should never let color override health, conformation, and temperament. Many people do, but this is a very short-sighted policy that can only result in problems.

TEMPERAMENT

Whether you want a hedgehog

as a pet or for breeding, its temperament, along with health, is the most important feature to consider. Unfortunately, it is also a feature that can be very difficult to evaluate. From a pet perspective, the way it handles may give you a good enough idea; indeed, this is the only basis for evaluation. From a breeding standpoint, assessing temperament based on a single specimen, especially a young adult, or mature individual, can be misleading. If a pet proves intractable, the chances are high that it will become an ignored pet. It will receive less general care and attention, so that it is more likely to become unhealthy as a direct result. Conversely, a hedgehog that is not as healthy as it should be, but that is very friendly, will quickly be given due veterinary care, and will thereafter be a delightful pet. These are the hard facts.

Hedgehogs are timid little animals at the best of times, which is why they have survived so well over thousands of years. Even a well-bred individual is cautious. However, when viewing potential pets, you should be able to gently lift one up, even if it is in a ball. It should then, within less than a minute, open up and allow you to handle it. If it does not, I would reject it. If it will allow you to stroke its forehead without undue problems, its temperament is good. If it will allow you to stroke its spines, and they are laid flat to its body, it is likewise a nice little animal. If it refuses to open up at all, it should be rejected as being unsuited to your needs, regard-

A defensive, frightened hedgehog, rolled tightly into a ball, is picked up in the same manner as a trusting one.

When a hedgehog is in this position, its spines feel much sharper, and you may wish to wear gloves in this case.

Even the best-bred hedgehog may initially be frightened by your touch. Ideally, it will open up within less than a minute.

less of what the seller tells you. I do not say that such an individual definitely has a poor temperament. Its problem may be environmental. But this you cannot determine, so it is best not to take a chance.

Environmental effect on temperament commences prenatally when the fetus is developing. Anything that negatively affects the mother may affect the offspring. This may be poor nutrition, stress, fear, poor health, and so on. Once a baby is born, the environment encompasses every aspect of its life.

The attitude of the mother will affect the youngster's attitude even before its eyes open. Thereafter, the environment will have a progressively greater impact on its life. A very well-bred youngster that is handled only rarely may appear much the same as a poorly bred individual. A hedgehog with a questionable genetic temperament can, with constant attention and loving care, appear to be a very tractable adult that is just a little shy.

A superbly bred hedgehog with a marvelous potential temperament can appear to be a real little monster if its upbringing is not as it should be—how are you to know which is which? This is why the pet owner should decide based on what he can *see* at the moment of purchase.

The potential breeder should not make decisions based on a single animal. Better that he sees a breeder's stock and assesses its overall worth, or obtains stock bred from a line that is known to be of very sound quality. If you are selecting from young breeding stock, try to see the litter(s) when it is about four weeks old. At this age (and earlier), temperament is showing itself in the individual. Some youngsters at this age show no fear whatsoever of humans; others are more timid. The latter ones may get better with constant handling but may regress if this is absent. The former will invariably stay tractable, even when ignored for periods of time.

An apparently good four- to eight-month-old young adult may

Close examination of this hedgehog reveals sparse spines and bald spots with patches of dry, flaky skin. This condition could be a health problem requiring veterinary care.

Look for bright eyes, a clean nose, and a clean rectum. Equally important is a friendly, trusting attitude.

Although partially rolled into a ball, this hedgehog shows an alert curiosity that bodes well for a new pet owner.

be masking a questionable on-ward breeding temperament due to excellent breeder care. All of its siblings may be the same, or it may be the one uncertain example from a litter of six. This is where the reputation of a breeder becomes so important, and why registered pedigrees are very useful in helping to trace quality stock and pinpoint problems in other lines.

HEALTH

There can be no reason ever to accept a pet that is less than 100 percent fit. Doing so can totally upset the pleasure that you had hoped for from your hedgehog. Matters are made difficult by the fact that not only does the hedge-hog mask ill health extremely well but also that many aspects of poor health are not at this time fully understood with this pet.

However, it is also true that a hedgehog is a very hardy animal. If you select wisely, the chances are heavily in your favor that your pet will lead a fully active and healthy life. Checking for signs of good health means you must be able to inspect the pet, so we come back to the question of it having a temperament that allows for this. You cannot inspect a pet that will not uncurl readily.

The eyes should be round and clear, with no evidence of being runny. The ears should be erect and show no suggestion of flakiness. The nose is small, smooth, and dry to just moist. It should not be discharging mucus or liquid, nor should the nostrils be swollen.

Inspecting the teeth is not always easy, but they should be small, white, and in a neat row, with none being out of alignment. It is possible that newly caged individuals, especially the more mature juvenile, may have a canine tooth missing. Such individuals may have literally extracted the tooth from its socket in an attempt to pull on the bars; or the tooth may be broken, in which case veterinary examination is recommended.

The fur should be soft and smooth to the touch. It should show obvious good condition, meaning it should be neither dry and lifeless, nor molting. Some individuals display a smoother fur than others, but this becomes apparent only if you view the stock of numerous breeders. The skin should be free of mites or other parasites, and there should be no bald patches, lumps, or abrasions.

The spines of youngsters are sharper than those of adults. There should be no areas of missing spines, other than for the

White hedgehogs are gaining in popularity. This well-bred, properly socialized specimen is easily handled.

narrow channel on the median line of the crown, this being normal for the species. The anal region should be clean and free of any signs of congealed fecal matter or staining, which would suggest a recent illness.

If the hedgehog looks rather drowsy or lethargic, this may be the result of one of two situations. It may indeed be ill. Alternatively, if the temperature is under 60° F., it may be entering a torpid state that precedes estivation.

A healthy hedgehog, when handled, will normally be very active, wanting to climb up your arm or body. Its nose is used extensively to sniff the air and pry your fingers apart to see what's behind them.

THE REASON FOR PURCHASE

The reason you wish to own a hedgehog will have some bearing on a number of aspects, including the source you go to for it. If you are purchasing a pet, your main considerations will be those of health, age, temperament, possibly color and sex, convenience of source, and finally price.

If you want breeding stock, your needs will of course include those for a pet. But you will also want to know much more about the ancestry of the stock you purchase than will the pet owner. Breeding stock should be obtained from a breeder of repute.

The pet owner may or may not be concerned about whether the stock is "papered", meaning if it has a pedigree, or if the pet can be registered. If you think this is not important, you should think again. If breeders go   to the trouble of preparing pedigrees and registering their breeding stock, it is because they value it. They are

Examination of the rectal area is essential. This animal shows evidence of both diarrhea and a rash. It should be in the care of an experienced breeder and a competent veterinarian, not in the hands of a first-time pet owner.

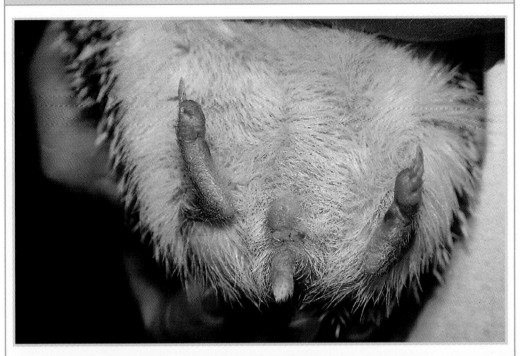

This is a female. The vulva is directly adjacent to the rectum.

concerned about breeding superior animals.

The breeder who simply wants to perpetuate hedgehogs at low cost can hardly claim to be producing quality if he has no records of his animals' matings. So, even if you want only a pet, you should insist that it comes with a pedigree. This document will tell you how old the animal is, its sex, and where it was bred. Purchasing non-papered animals merely encourages what is termed backyard breeding, where low cost, rather than quality, is the objective.

If you are delighted with your hedgehog and want another one just like it, you can ask your pet shop to obtain one for you from the same breeder, or from the same breeding lines. This is what pedigrees are for, and why they are so important.

PRICE

Hedgehog prices are as variable as prices for any other comparable pet. Even stock of similar quality and health may show regional and local price variation. There are numerous factors that control prices. These factors are related to the quality and temperament of the stock, the color and its relative scarcity, the availability of hedgehogs in a given area, and the breeder/seller's costs of producing/maintaining the animals and providing service to customers.

A breeder who has invested a large sum in his operation cannot offer stock at the low cost of a breeder who has little investment, has low standards, poor feeding regimens, and provides no paperwork or after-sales service. The only way you can assess market values is by checking with a *number* of sources, including the NAHA, which monitors prices nationally. Even from reputable sources, prices may fluctuate, as they will reflect the breeder's assessment of his animals' quality, their breeding worth, their age, or the breeder's need at that time to thin down surplus stock.

ASSESSING THE SUPPLIER

In any line of commerce, there are good and bad sources. If you end up with an unhealthy hedgehog with poor temperament, it is probable that you did not follow the advice noted below:

1. The premises from which hedgehogs are being sold should be clean, with no offensive odor.

2. The conditions under which the pets are being kept should be clean, with ample wood shavings to absorb fecal matter and urine. This is important with these pets.

Keeping hedgehogs on a few sheets of paper in a cage or aquarium is not satisfactory.

3. Food and water containers should be clean and not unduly worn, chipped, or scratched. Males and females should be in separate quarters. Water should be available at all times.

4. Hedgehogs need privacy and should therefore have in their quarters a small nesting box in which to retreat, or they should have rocks or logs against which they can curl up. Such furnishings screen them from any intense light and give them a sense of security.

5. The seller should be able to tell you the sex of each pet. If he cannot, he clearly knows little about these pets—hardly a good start!

6. The seller should be able to advise you on all aspects of feed-

What appears to be a belly button in the middle of the abdomen is actually the penis sheath of a male hedgehog.

A shy hedgehog may be sexed by viewing from underneath through a clear glass pie plate or bowl.

In addition to the animals themselves, pet shops will be able to supply you with housing, bedding, food, and utensils.

ing and basic care. If he cannot, it tells you that he has not taken the trouble to find out. Each hedgehog should come complete with its own feeding sheet so that you know what its regimen has been. Complete details of nutrition are given in this book. But because these pets can be finicky, it is important that you know what they have been eating. From this base, you can slowly adjust their diet.

7. If you purchase stock from sellers at an exotic animal exposition, do so only from those who will give you the address at which the hedgehogs are being bred, not just a PO box or a telephone number. Alternately, they will be members of the NAHA and can thus be traced in the event of problems.

I would not advise anyone to purchase from an animal auction, an open market, or similar places. Pet shops and breeders of repute are the *only* reliable sources for these pets.

8. Always be very wary of claims that you can make a fortune in no time with these pets. This may have been the case for a select few people when hedgehogs first started to take off as pets. It is definitely no longer the case.

A dedicated breeder of quality stock can turn a profit, but he will earn it the hard way and deserves the fruits of his own labors. The get-rich-quick merchants are now leaving the hobby to seek easy pickings in other exotics. The genuine breeders are now repairing the damage that unscrupulous breeders leave in their wake in all new pets.

THE MATTER OF GUARANTEES

Many people who contact associations ask if they should expect a guarantee when they purchase a pet. A hedgehog is not a mechanical item, or similar manufactured article. It is best compared to "perishable goods." How long a bag of fruit will last is very dependent on how you store it. A pet is very dependent on how it is fed and cared for. It can go down hill very rapidly if it is neglected, the more so the younger it is.

Although many pet owners will readily criticize pet shops and breeders, I can assure you that pet owners are often guilty of creating their own problems, then wanting the store or breeder to hand back money. They purchase a pet on impulse. When it proves to be unsuited to them, they will make all kinds of excuses as to why they should have a refund.

You should therefore regard a guarantee as a bonus and should not damn a supplier if he does not offer one. The seller cannot know whether you will care for the pet. Nor can he know what conditions you are keeping it under, or what pathogens (disease-causing organisms) it is being exposed to. It is up to you to be wholly satisfied as to the seller's genuineness, and the health of the pet, at the time you purchase the animal.

TRANSPORTING HEDGEHOGS

Hedgehogs readily suffer if conditions exceed the optimum conditions they need. In a lesser-of-two-evils situation, low temperature will be less dangerous to them over a short period (24 hours) than will excessive heat.

A defensive or frightened hedgehog will not unroll from a tight ball. In this position, it is impossible to examine the eyes, ears, rectum, or sex—not a good prospect for either the pet owner or the seller.

This means that if you transport a hedgehog in a vehicle during very hot weather, it is far more at risk of dying than if the temperature is on the cool side of its tolerance range.

Many hedgehogs have suffocated because they were left in vehicles when the temperature rose above 90° F., and there was no ventilation and water available to them. If the heat level drops below 55° F., they will become sluggish, depending on the ambient temperature at which they have formerly been kept. Warmth will generally return them to full activity within an hour or so.

You should therefore ensure that when transporting these pets, their container is well insulated, has adequate ventilation holes, the temperature is in the range of 60° to 75° F., and that the journey is made as quickly as is reasonably possible.

TRANSPORTING OVER LONG DISTANCES

If you wish to transport a hedgehog over a long distance, the container must be supplied with adequate dry food for the journey. It should also be supplied with a small gravity-fed water bottle that is securely fitted within it. Also include a nestbox, which should be securely attached to the floor.

This breeding facility shows care for the hedgehogs' environment.

Nutrition

Hedgehogs are very easy pets to care for in one respect, less so in another. They will take a wide-ranging diet, but they are very susceptible to obesity. They can also be rather finicky about sudden changes in their diet. We have discussed the feeding habits of these pets in the wild, so you already have a good idea of the range of foods they will eat.

However, we cannot provide an exact duplicate of their wild diet, nor would we want to. This would mean giving them food items such as carrion, which could be very unhealthy for them. In other instances, it would necessitate supplying items that some owners might prefer not to do on ethical grounds—pinky mice for example.

The diet must therefore be planned so that it provides all those foods containing the needed ingredients to ensure maximum and healthy growth, yet be readily available and convenient for the owner.

FOOD TYPES

Any food item can be viewed in various ways. It can be assessed on its protein, fat, or carbohydrate content, its vitamin value, its moisture content, or whether it's a "natural" food commercially prepared. We will discuss each of these elements, though not necessarily in this order. In doing so, you can come up with a suggested range of diets that should provide your pet with a well-balanced regimen.

Many hamster, gerbil, and bird utensils are suitable for use with hedgehogs.

The term *balanced* is worthy of attention because it does not always mean *varied.* A diet that contains a range of meats, their byproducts, and fruits would be varied, but it would not necessarily be balanced. It might not include certain items that are essential to the diet. It might also include some items that were not supplied in sufficient quantity for maximum growth and health.

Further, the fact that the animal is offered a varied diet does not mean it will always eat what is offered; it may prove to be highly selective, not always consuming the foods that it really should. There is thus an element of chance about any diet, it being a case that you must always be looking to reduce the chance element by observation, method of feeding, and experimentation.

A widely varied diet is most likely to meet your pet's nutritional needs.

MOISTURE CONTENT

Based on their moisture content, foods can be divided into three broad groups: moist, semi-moist, and dry. Examples, respectively, are live foods, prepared cat or dog foods, and commercial chow-type foods. Livefoods, such as invertebrates, and vegetables, which hedgehogs display little interest in, have a very high water content, as do items such as lean uncooked meats. They are often called "softfoods." Canned cat or dog foods range from high to medium-low in water content. Chow-type foods contain minimal moisture content.

The moisture content of the food will determine the amount of water your hedgehog will consume. The dryer the food, the greater the amount of water that is needed to compensate for its lacking in the food. However, even when fed a diet that includes good moisture content, these pets will still consume goodly quantities of water compared to other popular pets. Water must be available on an ad lib (free choice) basis. It must also be fresh.

In theory, low-moisture complete diets plus water are all that is needed. However, while such diets may be formulated to meet known metabolic needs, they do not address the psychological aspects of feeding, which can be very important. Any deficiency in this area will show itself in higher stress levels. Further, it should not be assumed that present knowledge of hedgehogs is such that all known important ingredients are indeed included in such foods, nor their most desirable ratio one to the other.

Chitin, the substance which is used in the formation of the exoskeleton of many invertebrates, may be lacking in needed quantities in formulated diets, especially in those prepared for cats or other small mammals.

Moist foods have a shorter shelf life compared to dry foods. Further, they more readily attract flies and other unwanted organisms. Each moist type of food will have its own level of palatableness to a pet, this being independent of what each contains, which will obviously have a high influence on the level of acceptance.

All of these facts suggest that you should feed a diet that includes items ranging from low to high in moisture content. This will provide foods that will help keep the teeth clean (dry foods), those which are readily digested (soft foods), and those that provide good jaw-muscle exercise (meats).

CONSTITUENTS OF FOODS

These are so well documented that only minimal introduction is needed.

Proteins are the building blocks of muscle, blood, brain and genes. They are required in greater quantity in growing youngsters, breeding sows, and those recovering from an illness, than those that are healthy non-breeding adults.

Activity level will also influence dietary needs. A pet that is free-roaming in the house, or lives in simulated-habitat accommodations, will burn up much more energy than one which is confined to long hours in a cage. Temperature will also influence protein needs. The lower it is, the more proteins will be needed to be converted to fatty tissue for insulation purposes.

Fats are required for many purposes, including insulation, and the transport of most compounds in the circulatory system. They also give food its taste. This

A treat of a few mealworms will be consumed with relish. Mealworms and other livefoods can be purchased at many pet shops.

said, hedgehogs do not assimilate fats readily and should not be given high-fat-content foods. This would rapidly result in obesity with its attendant problems, including poor blood circulation, inefficient body metabolism, reduced breeding capacity, and, almost certainly, reduced lifespan.

Carbohydrates provide the cheapest form of energy for day-to-day muscular activity. They provide fiber in various forms and are used by the body in many ways. Some carnivorous animals, such as dogs, are able to consume relatively large quantities of processed carbohydrates without adversely affected performance. Thousands of years under domestic conditions have improved their ability to cope with these compounds. The same is not nearly as true for cats, and even less so of hedgehogs.

These latter pets should be regarded as prime predators, even though their wild diet is essentially insectivorous. They need a high-protein diet. This means that prepared cat foods are superior to all but the best dog foods because of their higher protein content. Lean meats in their many forms are also desirable in either a raw or cooked state.

Vitamins are essential to all animals. Any deficiency in them (vitaminosis) will lead to various health and breeding problems. However, the same is true of excess vitamins (hypervitaminosis). As a general guide, you can decide whether or not vitamin supplements are beneficial based on the range of

This plate shows a normal-sized daily meal for a hedgehog.

Until a pet food manufacturer offers a complete, nutritionally balanced hedgehog ration, it is a good idea to include a small amount of natural feed in your hedgehog's daily diet.

foods your pet eats. If it is very limited, it would be wise to add a supplement.

If the pet has a wide-ranging diet, including commercially prepared vitamin-fortified foods, then there would be little to gain by adding supplements. Indeed, this is when excessive vitamin intake might occur. Mealworms include a good range of vitamins, as does liver.

The cooking of meats and other foods will greatly reduce their vitamin content. Likewise, vitamin supplements kept in warm or sunny locations will rapidly deteriorate, so keep them in cool (but not damp) darkened cupboards, a comment that is true for all perishable items.

Minerals are elements such as iron, copper, cobalt, iodine, cal-

cium, phosphorous, selenium, and manganese, to name but a few. They are required in small amounts and are found in all foodstuffs. Calcium is the one particular mineral that could be deficient in the diet and result in health problems for pets generally, as well as lactation difficulties for sows in particular. You can overcome this risk by sprinkling powdered calcium once a week over some of the food—just a very small amount. Alternatively, crushed egg shell, oystershell, or cuttlefish bone, mixed in with the regular meal or supplied in its own small dish, can be offered.

Reviewing the constituents of food, we can draw the following conclusions. The protein content should be high, the fat and carbohydrate levels relatively low. Vitamins and minerals should be given only if it is felt the diet lacks good variety and balance of one food type to the other.

LIVEFOODS

The only livefoods that you need to consider as being essential to your pet are invertebrates. The best examples are mealworms and crickets, but others include small earthworms, spiders, and crustaceans. These are very natural foods for your pet. They provide chitin, proteins, fats and a good range of vitamins. Livefoods are best obtained from a commercial source, as this dramatically reduces the risk that they will introduce parasites and the eggs or spores of pathogens to your pet. This would be the case with those gathered from the wild.

However, in foraging over a small part of your garden, your pet will delight in eating those beetles and larvae that it comes across. The risk of it ingesting potentially harmful parasites must be balanced against the benefits derived from the pet being able to forage in a very natural manner.

For the sake of convenience, you can purchase livefoods in frozen form. Make sure they are fully thawed before you serve them to your hedgehog. Nutritionally, frozen invertebrates and crustaceans are every bit as good as livefoods and are easier to keep. If they have a drawback, it is simply that they may not provide quite the same psychological stimulus to the pet. This can be

important to a hedgehog, especially when it is unwell or recovering from ill health and needs encouragement to eat.

Do not think that because these animals are insectivores they will be healthier if they are fed an exclusive diet of invertebrates. This is not the case. They may well be in the order Insectivora, but this is a man-made category. It is not an absolute guide to the nutritional needs of its members.

PLANNING A DIET

From the foregoing discussion, we can now look at a whole range of food items that you can supply to your pet so that its diet is both varied and balanced. In achieving balance, we must take a calculated guess. We still do not know the needed ratios of one food to another. Your guide will be in the health, activity level, and breeding capacity of your pet(s).

You can feed any meat that is lean, including beef, pork, lamb, poultry, and rabbit. Beware of lamb, especially, as it has a rather high fat content. Ground beef is well liked, but obtain the expensive grades—the cheap ones have high fat levels. As long as they are fit for human consumption, meats may safely be fed raw, or you can cook them. A little of each adds variety. If you are feeding chicken or its like, remove the skin after cooking—it is very fatty.

We ourselves have fed very little fish to our hedgehogs, but it is OK to feed them boiled (never raw) white fish in small amounts as an addition to the menu. You may also give your pet a small beef bone with some meat on it. The bone will be good exercise for its jaws and teeth. Avoid bones that splinter, such as poultry and rabbit. Liver is very rich in vitamins but must be fed sparingly, as it tends to give pets diarrhea.

Invertebrates of the various kinds discussed can be given daily, or on alternate days. You could give five mealworms each day or six to eight every other day. Although mealworms are the most easily obtained invertebrates,

A good-quality, dry cat kibble provides many important nutrients and also helps to keep the teeth clean.

Chopped hard-boiled eggs, low-fat cottage cheese, and beef extracts are other high-protein foods taken according to individual palate. One or more of these various meats and other high-protein foods should be included at *each* meal. Although some people give their hedgehogs a small amount of milk, or brown bread soaked in milk, this is not at all necessary and may result in diarrhea. Powdered milk is by far the better way to increase calcium content.

others, such as wingless insects, will be greatly appreciated and are worth obtaining as a change.

Mealworms can be kept for two to three months in your refrigerator. Place them in a plastic container that has a liberal amount of cornflower in it (regular white flour is too messy). If the worms are small, you can increase their size by placing a few pieces of lettuce or similar greens in the container for a short period of time before they are placed into the refridgerator. This they will eat. If you have a number of hedgehogs, it is economical to purchase them in large quantity.

Canned cat and dog foods are fortified with extra vitamins and also contain carbohydrates. Those that have a firm consistency, rather than the very moist ones, seem to be the most liked. Of the dry foods, the most popular are the better brands of complete cat diets, which come in a variety of flavors.

There is also a specially formulated hedgehog diet on the market. It appears to have a varying acceptance level, depending on which breeder is asked. Its formula is excellent, but, as with any complete diet, it should not be used exclusively. Some dry food should be included as part of every meal.

Hedgehogs show little interest in fruits and vegetables. Among those that are taken are apples, bananas, peaches, boiled potatoes, and raisins. These pets will also eat small amounts of high-quality alfalfa hay, as well as cauliflower and broccoli. We have tried a range of these foods with some success, and alfalfa seems to be the most popular for whatever reason. Some of that not eaten is invariably taken back as nesting material. With fruits, it may been that interest is centered on very ripe ones because they could contain small grubs.

It is grubs, rather than the fruit, that hedgehogs may be

These two plates of food demonstrate the different caloric requirements of hedgehogs. The small plateful would be an adequate feeding for a pet or non-stressed breeder while the large plateful would be only a portion of the daily feeding required by a lactating female with a large litter.

Generally speaking, fruits and vegetables do not rank high on the list of hedgehogs' favorite foods.

eating when reportedly eating fruit in the wild. Do not worry unduly if your pet refuses fruits and vegetables, but keep trying small amounts so it has the opportunity to become familiar with them. You can try samplings of grain and bird seeds, as well as various nuts, such as unsalted peanuts; but it may take a while before a taste for them will be acquired, if at all.

By including a meat, maybe a byproduct, and a complete-diet dry food at every meal, you ensure a representative range of important nutrients. The addition of invertebrates daily, or on alternate days, should ensure adequate balance. A drop of cod-liver oil once per week, or a vitamin supplement, added to the meat will ensure a good intake of vitamins if they are thought to be necessary.

FOOD PRESENTATION

There are three basic ways in which you may offer the hedgehog its food. Each has its own advantage.

1. Serve a variety of foods in the same dish, but do not mix them together: let the pet be selective. By this means, you are not only able to observe which foods are appealing but also you will be able to determine the order in which they are preferred. This can be important when introducing a new item, or when coaxing an unwell pet to maintain its food intake.

In the former case, you can withhold a favored item for 24

hours and replace it with an alternate (but one of similar feeding value). The pet will tend to go for its second favorite first, but may well then try the new item because it is not yet satiated. At the next meal, you return its favorite food but add just a little of the new item as well. By this means, the hedgehog's "taste" can be acquired for a range of foods. This is very important in correct diets.

2. You can prepare a mash of foods. Take the various ingredients and chop them into tiny pieces. The pet is not able to be quite so selective and may therefore acquire a taste for a new item added in very small quantity. (It is important that the quantity of the newly added food is small; otherwise, the pet may reject most of the food.

It is best to feed your pet mashes only when you have some idea of which foods your pet will eat, and in what kind of ratio. You can then prepare larger quantities and keep enough for a few days in the refrigerator. Be very sure to feed all foods at room temperature, never chilled.

3. Dry foods and invertebrates can be scattered in an open area of the pet's habitat or cage. This has the advantage that the hedgehog can obtain part of its diet in a very natural manner. It will enjoy using its strong scenting powers and foraging inclinations to seek out food items. Don't worry that the item may disappear beneath the shavings—your pet will find it. However, if invertebrates are placed too near to heavy rocks, they may creep under the rocks,

where your pet cannot get at them. Each day lift the rock(s) to see if any have done this. Simply place them elsewhere for the pet to find.

NUMBER OF MEALS AND QUANTITY OF FOOD

Insectivores are foraging creatures. This means that in the wild they do not consume a single large meal and then retire to digest it. Rather, they actively feed over a period of about twelve hours. That most breeders feed their stock an appropriate amount only once per day (as does this author at this time) is a matter of convenience for them, rather than one of correctness from the hedgehog's viewpoint.

The number of meals you give your pet each day will reflect the time your are able to devote to it, and whether or not you are able to change its activity period as discussed in the previous chapter. If possible, it is suggested that two meals a day are better than one large one. This will encourage an increased activity level, and a better digestive schedule for the pet.

For example, when you return home from work you can give it a small meal and provide the main meal just before you retire at night. Alternatively, give it the main meal mid-evening—about 8pm—and provide a small meal early in the morning if you are an early riser. Your pet will adjust to whatever schedule you make, as long as you are consistent in it.

With regard to quantity, this is always difficult to determine because no two hedgehogs are quite the same. As a *very* approximate guide, one to two ounces of mixed food (dry, meat, and invertebrates) per day should be sufficient to keep a typical pet in good health.

It is not the quantity of food so

little extra. If a lot is left at the first meal, reduce the quantity at the next. Your ideal is when the pet leaves maybe a few items that will be eaten at its later leisure.

Feeding is not an exact science, nor can it ever be. It is a case that

Hedgehogs spend most of their waking hours exploring, most likely looking for the next bite of food.

much as its quality that is important. The lesser the quality the greater the quantity needed to provide the required nutrients. The trial-and-error system is as good as any to determine the amount needed. With this method, you place a quantity of varied items for the pet to eat. If the food is greedily devoured within five minutes, you have not supplied enough, so give a

you must learn by observation of your pet whether or not it is clearly healthy, active, and displaying good color, skin, and spines. Moist perishable foods should be removed after a few hours—never leave them to sour.

FINICKY PETS

A problem that often arises when pets are obtained from

sellers that have maintained their stock on a Spartan diet is that the new owner finds that some of the foods we have discussed are rejected. Sometimes the unfamiliar will be ignored; sometimes it will be ravenously eaten. Each hedgehog is an individual, a fact that should never be forgotten.

Some pets will literally starve rather than try unfamiliar foods if this is all they are given. Never attempt to change a diet suddenly, but do it as discussed: a little at a time. If an item that you know is good for it is ignored, offer it again and again. It may be that your newly acquired pet is stressed, so it will eat only the minimum that its body needs. Once it settles down, it may be more willing to try new items as its activity level, thus appetite, increases.

OBESITY AND THINNESS

It is already apparent in the short history of this pet that both obesity and thinness are problems facing many owners. However, there is also a tendency for breeders to regard these extremes in a rather simplistic manner—overfeeding and underfeeding, which would seem the obvious reasons for these conditions.

This is by no means always the case. Some hedgehogs, like many other pets, are "easy keepers." This means that even on very Spartan rations, some individuals will still become rather obese. Likewise, some animals, regardless of how much they eat, will remain slim, even skinny.

Further, the bodily condition in some individuals is related to their age as much as to their food intake. We have found in our Camelot stud that certain "hefty" females have a tendency to produce offspring of their own ilk. In other words, the problem is genetic. Lack of exercise is also a contributory factor in some instances. Excess weight may also be due to a metabolic malfunction, a situation that would require veterinary counsel. One way or the other, the matters of obesity and thinness are not always problems about which you can make rapid or definitive judgment.

Nonetheless, if your pet is overweight or too thin, your first line of thought should be directed to the diet—assuming it is not the case, with a female, that she is pregnant! If the pet is overweight, you must weigh it, so that you have a figure for the sake of comparison.

Prepare a normal meal and weigh it, making notes on what its content are. Next, contact the breeder or your vet and discuss the matter. Never attempt crash diets with pets: doing so can be dangerous. Any dieting must be done gradually. Be sure no fatty foods are in the diet. Reduce the quantity of the food but retain the same varieties so that nothing is missing. It can take weeks or months before results will be apparent. Ensure that the hedgehog is getting ample exercise. Slimming these pets is not easily done, so it is better that the situation is avoided where possible.

To do this, you should weigh your pet when you obtain it and take monthly readings. Its weight will rise steadily until it is about six months old (but maybe longer), when it will start to level off. If you notice its weight is continuing to climb, then is the time to start adjusting the diet, before the pet becomes obese. If lack of weight is the problem, gradually increase the amount of food and monitor the weight gain.

This domestic hedgehog instinctively knows that woodpiles are a good source of insects and protection.

Foraging is natural behavior, and these animals will pick up crumbs and odd objects from the carpet. Do not allow the hedgehog to roam areas that have been treated with insecticides or chemicals.

Housing

Your hedgehog should be supplied with housing that reflects its natural needs as far as possible. This means that you can never provide too much space, but you can certainly provide too little. The entire subject of accommodations is very subjective, depending on your views of the freedom any animal has a born right to be given.

There is no doubt that any animal can live a healthy life, and breed, within the confines of a relatively small cage. But to say that it is leading a contented, or even desirable, life is another matter. Hedgehogs are very active little animals that, at times, like to be on the move almost continually. They enjoy investigating things, and they also like to clamber up and down obstacles.

While they will indeed readily drink from a water bottle if that is their only option, they much prefer to drink from an open pot that allows them to swallow as nature intended. They are fossorial animals, which means they like to forage over the ground for food items. They enjoy rolling over in dust baths, which is probably how they remove pests in the wild, much as do dogs, cats, horses and their like.

Each of these needs means that their accommodations should allow these natural activities to be completed. It is unfortunate that the hedgehog hobby grew rapidly

out of an investor market that was based on housing as many breeding animals as possible within the least amount of space. As a consequence, the use of small cat carry crates and their like became, and remain at this time, the "standard" method of housing them.

This does not mean that this is the ideal way to house hedgehogs, though I have no doubt that it is the least costly way to accommodate large numbers of breeding stock, as it is in rabbits, guinea

Most hedgehogs will select one corner of their enclosure for a latrine. Placing a litter tray in that corner reduces cleaning time. Normal hedgehog feces should be small and firm with a consistent color.

pigs, and most other small animals. For the pet owner, the use of a small-sized housing unit is justified only if it is a place for the pet to sleep, and maybe feed. The pet must be given liberal out-of-cage time in which to exercise and explore.

For the potential breeder, the use of cages, coupled with limited space, may well dictate some cage accommodations. But breeders should have areas where their stock, on a rotational basis, is allowed to enjoy recreational activities. Better still would be to reduce the number of animals kept so that they could all be given greater space than is presently the case.

In point of fact, the rapid reduction in hedgehog prices came about specifically because breeders were overproducing relative to the size of the market. The policy of keeping large numbers of these pets in confined spaces has thus detracted from their investment value. It will continue to do so for as long as cage breeding is practiced on a large scale, as a number of breeders are now realizing.

In the following discussion, we will therefore consider the needs of the hedgehog as paramount. Then, from a breeder perspective, we will examine how the breeding room can be so organized as to meet the needs of controlled production and the hedgehog's welfare. The hedgehog's spatial needs should dictate the numbers kept—rather than the other way 'round!

CAGES

The term "cage" can be applied to a carry crate, an aquarium, any of the small mammal and rabbit cages, or any structure that offers limited space in which to create a home environment, but which will not allow the pet to gain ample exercise.

This wire-type enclosure is fine for pets or studs but will not provide the feeling of privacy required by a breeding female.

The basic requirements for a cage are that it is very easy to clean, has no dangerous metal projections, and has sufficient space for a nestbox, food dishes, and a latrine area. It should then have sufficient space for the pet to move between these items. This means that the floor area should be no less than about 51 x 28cm (20 x 11 in.). This would be a very small area for these pets to live in, so it should be regarded as the very minimum and best suited to the pet that is allowed ample time out of its cage.

Height is less important than floor area but should be in excess of 25cm (10 in.) so that the pet can stretch upward to its full length and have some space over its snout. Cages fitted with metal cross bars are the least suitable form of cage. It is quite possible for a hedgehog to get a nail caught on a cross bar as it clambers up the bars. It may not be able to release itself. Its leg may then get twisted, with obvious pain and injury being the result.

Any fully enclosed cage, such as an aquarium, must have ample ventilation holes to ensure a good supply of air, and for odors to escape. The carry crates that have a raised lip where the door opens are useful because they keep the substrate from falling out—a problem with cages in which the door is at floor level.

In a larger cage, it is possible to construct a bi-level platform with a connecting ramp. This almost doubles the floor area and enables

This habitat is large enough to accommodate a dustbath, waterbath, and nestbox—with space left over for exercise.

Many pet owners build custom wooden homes for their hedgehogs. Wood should be very well sealed, or it will absorb urine and be a constant source of odor.

you to place food and sleeping quarters in the upper level, leaving the lower level free for an exercise area and toilet space.

ECOSYSTEM (HABITAT) HOUSING

Ecosystem housing offers many advantages over traditional cages. The most important of these is obviously that the pet is given greater space in which to move around. This reduces potential stress levels. Ecosystem housing enables two or more females to be kept together, and it allows you infinite flexibility in its furnishings. It is this author's view that such habitats are more hygienic and encourage greater interaction between owner and pet because

most will be open topped, so access is instant.

Further, you feel happier that your pet is living a fuller life rather than one that is very restrictive. It is difficult to enthuse on how to upgrade a cage, but a mini habitat is altogether different. It can be furnished in a number of interesting ways.

From the breeder's viewpoint, time devoted to routine chores is actually less than would be the case with a number of cages. Further, a carefully planned ecosystem can offer the breeder very flexible usage.

SIZE

The size of an ecosystem will be determined by whether it is to be a portable or a fixed unit. A micro habitat will have an area of about 124 x 62cm (48 x 24in.) but can be somewhat smaller. Such a unit, even when furnished, can be moved from one site to another by two people. A mini habitat will range up to 124 x124cm (48 x 48 in.), while a standard habitat will be anything larger than the mini system.

The author's largest hedgehog habitat is presently 12 x 4 ft., thus offering a floor area of 48 sq.ft. This easily accommodates ten non-breeding females and could house more without any problems. A habitat can, of course, be narrow and long, and it can also be two-tiered in part or whole to create even more space. Sizes will be standardized by the NAHA for exhibition purposes. Such habitats will greatly increase the appeal of hedgehog exhibitions for many exhibitors, as well as for the public.

CONSTRUCTION

At this time there are no commercially made habitats, but they will no doubt appear in due course. All-glass terrariums are available, but they are rather costly and must be specially ordered. Most owners will therefore be building their own.

The prerequisites for an ecosystem unit are that it has a strong floor to take the weight of decorations, has side walls with a height of no less than 31cm (12 in.) to prevent the pet's escaping, and can be readily cleaned. Ideally, the floor and walls should be melamine-coated timber. The alternative is to be sure that the wood is well painted with a non-toxic washable paint. The floor can be covered with a quality linoleum.

Given that hedgehogs are able climbers, the side walls should be solid rather than of weldwire or its like. From a viewing and servicing standpoint, we have found that the most desirable height of the habitat floor from the room floor is 71-76cm (28-30 in). This has been arrived at after constructing numerous units at different heights. It also is a good height for those who wish to breed their hedgehogs.

It is worth the extra time and small cost to have the walls (or, at least the front one) made so that they slide between their supporting pillars, thus are removable. This will make cleaning and rearranging furnishings much easier, especially in the larger units.

PLANNING THE BREEDING ROOM

Planning a breeding room using ecosystems can easily be done by featuring divider panels every two feet along a given length of habitat. For example, if the length of the unit is 16 x 4 ft., this has a potential of eight 4 x 2 ft. units, four 4 x 4 ft. units, and so on. A 4 x 4 ft. unit will comfortably accommodate two to four non-breeding females. The 16-ft. unit divided into four will house up to 16 non-breeding females, all of which could equally be kept in the one large 16-ft. spread.

You can feature another unit beneath the main unit. However, in this case, it is best to construct four independent units that are equipped with casters. This allows them to be pulled out for ease of cleaning. Each of these units can again be divided into two by using slider panels. They will not be quite four feet wide because of the upright supports to the main ecosystem above them, which they must clear when they are pulled out.

the shelving can feature night/day lighting.

Within a 16 x 10 ft. building or room, this still leaves adequate space for a refrigerator, work areas, and indeed another somewhat smaller two-tier habitat system. Such an arrangement should prove adequate for the small-scale breeder.

FLOOR COVERING

Regardless of the type of housing, the recommended floor cover-

Wire cages provide ease of cleaning and a good view of your hedgehog's antics, but care must be taken in their selection. Beware of sharp edges and spaces that could trap a hedgehog's head or leg.

Presupposing that one unit is always 8 ft. wide and used as a main display habitat, this still leaves considerable system flexibility of up to twelve 4 x 2 ft. units if needed. Further, there is sufficient space above the main unit to place storage shelves if required. The space underneath

ing is commercially produced white pine shavings. Do not try to cut costs by obtaining shavings from lumberyards or other sources, because there is a high risk that you will introduce mites to your pets.

If you wish to add an extra touch of greenery to the substrate, you can sprinkle some chlorophyll-impregnated shavings on the surface. The depth of the shavings should be about one inch so that they will soak up urine.

Sawdust should not be used because it is too fine and can cause irritation to the eyes, underparts, and ears. Other unsuitable floor coverings are garden soil, hay, straw, and newspaper (though in the granulated form this is more acceptable).

NESTBOX

Your pet should be supplied with a suitable nestbox in which to retreat when it so wishes. Possibilities for a nestbox include the following for a cage or habitat.

A one-gallon tote box turned upside down so the lid is on the floor. A hole is cut in the front to facilitate an entranceway, which need only be large enough for the pet to walk through.

Other possibilities include a plastic office-trash can (this is suited only to the large cage or habitat); a large-diameter (4 in. or more) plastic pipe with both ends left open; a parakeet nestbox with the hole enlarged.

For the habitat, your options are greater. You can fashion rocks and logs so that they create a cave-type dwelling. In a habitat setting, hedgehogs will not always use the nestbox and are quite happy to snuggle up to a log if it is in a cozy corner; or they will

A browse through your local pet shop will provide you with many options for housing.

The cage should provide your pet with ample room to walk around.

retreat behind a suitably large rock. You can place a covering of shavings in the nestbox; but if the room temperature is adequate, they will invariably push bedding material out of the box, or to the front opening, unless they are breeding females with a litter.

FOOD AND WATER CONTAINERS

For the cage, a gravity-fed water bottle is the most popular water dispenser because it takes up no internal room, remains dust free, and will last two to three days before it needs replenishing.

Open water pots are always a preferred choice; but in a confined space, they must, of necessity, be small. The pet can overturn a small water pot, soaking the immediate flooring. This, of course, is not desirable.

However, if the pet is allowed ample "free" time in a room, you can place a heavy water dish just outside the cage. In this way, the pet has access to its water and its cage stays dry. In a habitat, the open pot, while more labor intensive, is the best choice. It must be heavy, or surrounded by rocks so that it cannot be tipped over.

Feeding dishes can range from saucers to cat bowls to small crock pots. We use the double plastic cat bowls in our habitats, so a number of hedgehogs can feed at the same time. Space limitations in the average cage invariably mean that the food dish will be overturned and walked over unless it can be secured.

Nestboxes will also be moved because the hedgehog wants to check what is underneath them.

Litter pans can be included in a large cage. Your pet will use them, or one corner of its accommodations if an easy-access pan is not provided.

CAGE AND HABITAT FURNISHINGS

It is very difficult within a cage already supplied with a food dish, nestbox, and, perhaps, a litter pan to include other items without the unit being so cluttered that there is no room for the hedgehog to move around. Only in a very large cage should other items be included. The habitat, however, lends itself to unlimited scope, depending on its size. The following are some ideas that may be possible in your pet's home.

1. Rocks. Slate, granite, and hard sandstone are the best, but most natural rocks can be utilized to create interesting furnishings. They can be of various shapes and sizes. Even house bricks can be fashioned into cave-like nestboxes. They can also be sealed and painted so that they are easily washed.

2. Logs. Split and whole logs are a very natural furnishing for hedgehogs. They can be arranged so that the pet can easily clamber on and off of them. They will especially clamber about during the night, when you are probably asleep.

Along with logs, you can often gather interesting pieces of dry wood that make excellent decorations. All rocks, logs, and decorations should be disinfected before being used. This is done by immersing them for two minutes in a bucket of water containing one-half cup of household bleach. They are then dipped into another bucket containing clean water and hosed to remove residual chemicals. Finally, they are then left to dry before being used. By collecting a variety of these "props," you always have a sufficient supply to rotate and ensure periodic cleansing.

3. Plastic plants. These decorations can be very effective in creating a natural look in a habitat. They can be readily cleaned. They need to be large enough so that they can be secured; otherwise, your pet may drag them to its nestbox entrance.

4. Wooden decorations. If you are handy, you can make interesting nestbox decorations—from castles to adobe homes—for your pet. You can make bridges that your pet will walk over, while using the underpart as a nestbox. You can make miniature gardens and similar scenes. You are limited only by available space and your imagination.

The main thing to bear in mind when designing a habitat is that it must always be arranged so that you can easily get at each hedgehog living in it. It should also be relatively easy to disassemble and disinfect. Ensure that there is a pathway that enables the pet to run around, as well as items to climb up and down in safety.

5. "Rolling" Box. If you supply your pet with an easily accessed box containing very small gravel,

the kind used for aquariums, mixed with commercial potting soil, you will witness something that most pet owners and breeders do not see.

The hedgehog will go into the box and start to roll over with obvious enjoyment. It will usually do this after it has eaten. After a few rolls and shakes, it will leave the box. This is no doubt a natural means of cleansing that is practiced in its wild habitat. If a number of females are kept, two or three will do this at the same time.

given more than normal consideration in this chapter because of its importance to pet owners and future breeders. Most of what has been said is correct as applied to the breeder who has stated it, but it may not be the full picture for every hedgehog.

This means that if these pets are subjected to extended periods when they are maintained at a constant temperature within their natural range of acceptable temperatures, they will tend to react negatively to any sudden change.

For example, if you were to keep

The larger the housing unit the more accessories you will be able to provide.

TEMPERATURE REQUIREMENTS

There has been a great deal said and written about the temperature needs of African pygmy hedgehogs. This topic is therefore

your hedgehog in a room where the constant heat was 77° F., it is very likely that if this heat was then dropped to 70° F., and almost certainly to 65° F., the pet would contract a chill and become torpid. If, however, the pet was normally maintained at 68° F., it would not necessarily have a reduced activity level, nor be at risk to chilling. This would be apparent at a lower temperature.

In other words, the important factor is not that a specific temperature *per se* is required, but rather that it should be constant, or within a given range of fluctuation over any 24-hour period.

It is this author's firm belief that to maintain a constant temperature throughout the year for these hedgehogs, as is presently often done, can and will result in stock of low vigor and greater susceptibility to the most minor of health problems. It is of little merit to claim to be breeding only the most vigorous adults when they are so cocooned that it is quite impossible for vigor to be fully displayed.

Earthenware food bowls are a good choice because they do not tip and can be easily cleaned.

There is also no doubt that natural vigor is masked under domestic conditions that ensure that less vigorous offspring survive than would be the case in the wild. This is reinforced when temperatures are maintained at high levels throughout the year, rather than being allowed to fluctuate with the seasons.

To underscore this point, one need only look at certain other pets, such as cage birds, to see that certain controlled breeding room strains keel over when they are placed under outdoor aviary conditions. This is not to imply that you should be casual or less than serious in controlling the temperature, but neither should you become paranoid in maintaining a specific heat or humidity level for your hedgehog, and especially so for breeding stock.

With these considerations in mind, the following guidelines should be useful. The temperature range in which this species will remain active under domestic conditions can be safely regarded

A hedgehog given ample exercise space will most certainly be able to cope with temperature fluctuations far better than the caged pet. A pet kept under conditions that display a two- to five-degree fluctuation over a 24-hour period (which would be quite normal in the average home) will usually be more vigorous than one kept under a constant tem-

Use common sense in selecting an enclosure. Safety is the first concern, followed by adequate size and ease of cleaning.

as 65 to 80° F.(18.3 to 26.7° C). Anything above or below this level is probably uncomfortable for the hedgehog and may well induce stress and ill health if the hedgehog is maintained in a small cage. The preferred optimum appears to be 68 to 74° F. if a narrow range is to be stated.

perature for the same period of time.

Once the overnight outdoor temperature is consistently above 45° F. and the daytime temperature is above 55° F., the breeder could begin to lower the breeding room temperature over a period of three to four weeks. In other words, during the warmer months the outdoor temperature is what determines the breeding room heat level, but maybe with a control applied to prevent it going much over 80° F. The occasional overnight dip below 50° F. should not adversely affect a strong healthy hedgehog. If it does, this suggests the individual is lacking in vigor.

Keep in mind that temperature is affected by altitude: the higher the altitude, the lower the temperature. Humidity and wind chill factors will also influence temperature. All of these interacting influences mean that even within a single species, local populations will display variability in their optimum range when compared to populations from another area (country).

When a breeder artificially creates an environment, which includes its weather, retention of vigor is vital because the stock that he sells will be going to homes where a very narrow range of temperature fluctuation is unlikely to found. The stock must be capable of adjusting to a reasonable fluctuation in temperature range; otherwise, the new owners may quickly experience problems.

LIGHTING AND ITS CYCLES

In their native habitat, the African hedgehogs experience a day/night cycle of about even length—12 hours of each. Under domestic conditions, they display no problems in adjusting to some variation in this cycle. Although nocturnal, they can also adjust to being more active during daylight hours than would be the case in the wild.

Housing for small mammals such as hedgehogs is reasonably priced to meet the most modest budget.

Hedgehogs are happiest when given free run of the house. Very few people are able to adequately hedgehog-proof their entire home, and so they give their pet access to just one room.

However, they should not be subjected to intense brightness, neither outdoors nor indoors, especially outdoors during peak sunshine periods. In the breeding room, there should be some natural daylight, that from skylights being the most space economical insomuch as it does not take up wall space as do windows.

During the winter months, it is advantageous to feature a rheostat (dimmer) so that some control can be placed on the light/dark cycle. A rheostat allows the lighting to come on and go off in a gradual manner, rather than suddenly, thus avoiding light or night fright, which tends to startle the pets and increases stress levels.

The alternative to this, if it will be dark before you arrive home, is to use any of the light-sensitive bulbs that come on as it reaches a certain level of darkness. You could also switch on a low-wattage bulb before you leave home to achieve much the same effect.

The use of lights in the blue spectral range, to simulate moonlight, is useful if you have habitat-type housing and wish to quietly observe your pet's activities under subdued lighting. Indeed, given the nocturnal penchant of these pets, various soft-colored lighting options can be used with imagination in or around the pet's housing.

OTHER USEFUL APPLIANCES

There are a number of products

now available that the breeder in particular will find useful. Certainly, an exhaust fan in the breeding room will be obligatory in order to continually remove stale air.

The use of an ionizer will likewise be of great help in controlling dust, airborne pathogens, and odors. These units come in a range of sizes and are economical to run. They should be run continually for best results. They produce millions of negative ions that attract dust and other particles, making them heavier than air. The dust and other particles fall to the floor or other surfaces, where they are more easily removed during regular cleaning.

In the warmer climates, a cooling system will make life more comfortable for both owner and hedgehogs by limiting the upper temperature. With regard to heating, we have found that propane is considerably less costly than electric in the breeding room.

Be sure, however, that whatever form of heat is used, its level is controlled via a thermostat. Doing so will help to prevent temperature-related problems.

ROUTINE MANAGEMENT

As with any animal, you can avoid costly vet bills by ensuring that the conditions under which your pet lives are such as to minimize the likelihood of pathogenic colonization of the housing, thus the hedgehog.

Cages should be routinely cleaned each day to the degree that all fecal matter is removed. Complete replacement of floor covering is a weekly necessity, at which time the nestbox and other furnishings should also be disinfected, then rinsed. Habitat housing, based on its size, will survive a longer period before it needs to be completely stripped and cleaned, depending on how many hedgehogs it houses. But fecal matter should still be removed on a daily basis. Breeders should never leave soiled floor material in the breeding room. It should be removed as soon as cleaning is completed.

Food dishes should be cleaned every day, as should open water pots. Bottle water dispensers should be cleaned every week and checked daily to see if they are dispensing water.

Every time you handle your hedgehog, it should be inspected for any signs of mites, which are probably the most common parasite to affect this pet, depending on the source of its floor material and the level of hygiene maintained. Watch for cuts, abrasions, or lumps, which should be promptly attended to so that they get no worse, nor provide sites for secondary infection. Be very sure that all foods are kept under ideal conditions (cool, dry, dark) and that only fresh foods are ever given to the pet. If you have any doubt about the freshness of a food item, it is best to discard it.

It is not necessary to bathe your pet unless it is being treated for a parasitic problem. Hedgehogs kept under clean conditions will remain clean and odor free.

A custom-built enclosure can provide ample room for the hedgehog and viewing pleasure for the owner.

Breeding Theory

It requires no special efforts or skill, other than those related to management, to place sexually willing male and female hedgehogs together and let nature take its course. Such hobbyists who practice this method of reproducing the species hardly qualify for the title of "breeder" in any worthwhile meaning of the word.

To compound matters, many who call themselves breeders made no special effort to obtain healthy typical examples of these animals before embarking on their breeding programs. The proof of this statement is seen in many of the unhealthy, bad-tempered, and poor-mothering females now in existence.

The fact is that many breeders in this young hobby commenced with no real desire, or knowledge, to conduct a breeding program, but did so only in order to cash in on what was initially a very lucrative investment. It mattered not what the offspring were like, only that as many as possible could be produced and reared to be sold as investment "breeding" stock.

The decline in prices brought about by mass producing more youngsters than there was a market for was both inevitable, and, in a way, beneficial to the long-term interests of the hobby. Low prices rapidly remove the leeches from hobbies. This then allows the serious hedgehog enthusiasts to steadily build up quality herds from which future breeders can buy in confidence.

Some breeders are working to produce specialty colors like this lovely white specimen with dark ears, eyes, and muzzle.

Some in the hobby concentrate on producing the very best temperament in the standard agouti-colored animals.

RESEARCH THE INITIAL STOCK

Sound breeding strategy begins before you even mate your stock. It costs no more to feed quality hedgehogs than it does to feed poor specimens of the species. The latter will only produce their own kind unless you attempt to upgrade subsequently by obtaining better stock to pair with them. But this can be a long process, so it is financially expedient to commence with sound stock from the outset.

Make numerous inquiries to breeders of repute to see what the going rate is for breeding stock of the variety and age you want. Your stock must be pedigreed; otherwise, its offspring's value will automatically be lower. Your initial cost of stock is but a fraction of your long-term costs, so it really does make good sense to purchase your hedgehogs from a well-established breeder.

LIMIT INITIAL NUMBERS

Do not go out and purchase, as some have done, a large number of individuals. This is the reason prices fell so sharply in hedgehogs after a brief period of unrealistically high prices. Start out on a small scale, as this offers you several advantages. It enables you to devote the essential time needed to socializing the babies, which is vital in this hobby, and for your future reputation. It gives you time to develop practical

The first meeting between male and female is tense.

breeding skills and to determine whether or not your initial stock is producing good healthy offspring. It also gives you the time in which to decide whether being a breeder really is of lasting appeal to you. Many people who begin breeding pets soon become disenchanted after the initial wave of enthusiasm and vanish from the hobby they are in.

An adequate start would be no more than two to three females, one of which should be unrelated to the other two. A boar is not needed at this level unless you are so isolated that access to a boar would be costly. However, even this you can easily overcome by purchasing two bred females. A good boar can be retained from each of their litters to be used on the females it is not related to.

RECORD KEEPING

Crucial to any breeding program will be accurate records. Without them, it would be quite impossible to plan and effect a program. From your records, you can often trace genetic problems and virtues, decide which individuals to mate, and establish what is variable, normal, or abnormal within your herd. Based on this collective data, you are better positioned to decide when, if, and what kind of individuals you may need to improve your program.

Records fall into two basic types. There are the individual records of each hedgehog, and there are the collective records that can be kept by category. The latter might be breeding, medical evaluation, or any other aspect

BREEDING THEORY

that you might wish to log. The more data you have the better. But the extent of it should reflect the amount of time you have available to devote to this area of management. It is better to keep minimal records and have them complete, than to attempt too much and not keep them up to date.

INDIVIDUAL HEDGEHOG RECORDS

Basic information should include the following: name of hedgehog, registration number or other identification number, sex, date of birth, color (including genetic state, if known), sire and dam, birth date, date of death (longevity), length and weight at given ages, number of times mated, number of offspring pro-

duced per litter, breeder, purchase price, and general notes (weak features, etc.).

A photograph or drawing of the individual's markings is very useful, indeed essential, if you want to breed given patterns. It will help you to draw conclusions with respect to the *possible* mode of inheritance if this has not been established as a fact.

BREEDING RECORDS

The breeding records give you at-a-glance information about your entire program. They should indicate the name of the sow, her ID number, who she was mated to, and when. The gestation period will be noted, along with the number of offspring, their sexes, and colors.

Temperament and disposition, as evidenced by handleability, should be given more consideration in the breeding program than should fancy color.

99

Any problems experienced with rearing, deaths, and so on should also appear on this record. Breeding records can be individual to the sow, or they can be collective, meaning covering a number of sows based on mating dates, or whatever. If youngsters are fostered to other sows, this must be noted. Your other records, such as medical, feeding, and so on, are planned in much the same manner, so that you have a complete series of case histories for all of your stock.

THE PEDIGREE

It is a fact that breeders of many kinds of pets will decry the value of pedigrees on the grounds that "they prove nothing and are useful only to those who show their stock." This is rubbish and merely indicates that the person who says such a thing has virtually no knowledge of what sound breeding is all about—and none on what a pedigree is all about. Even a pet hedgehog should have a pedigree; otherwise, you will know nothing about it.

A pedigree is an important document that should never be overestimated or underestimated in its value. Just how valuable it is will be determined by a) the knowledge of the reader, b) the amount of research they are prepared to do in abstracting information from the pedigree, and c) what information is given in this document.

Space limits detailed discussion of pedigrees, but the following are

Some hedgehogs will get along with other pets in the family; others, like this prickly little ball of spines warding off the family feline, do not.

Sexing is relatively easy in hedgehogs. The female's vulva is right above the rectal opening. Prior to breeding, each female should be given a visual check for abnormal mammary glands, rashes, or external parasites.

points that you should be aware of:

1. A pedigree indicates the *line* of descent, not necessarily its quality or purity.

2. A pedigree is only as good as the hedgehog that bears it. A mediocre hedgehog with the most outstanding pedigree bearing the names of the most famous breeders and hedgehogs is still a mediocre hedgehog—and will breed that way. An outstanding individual of no particular merit in its pedigree is still outstanding and will probably pass on at least some of its features to its offspring.

3. The most important generations in a pedigree are the parents and grandparents. An individual will receive exactly 50 percent of

its genes from its sire and dam. This is fact. In theory, it will have received 25 percent of its genes from its grandparents: this is general theory rather than fact because it may not have received 25 percent of the genes of a given grandparent. It could have received 0 to 25 percent, indeed 0 to 50 percent.

Likewise, it would be foolhardy to assume that 12.5 percent of its genes represent those of its great grandparents, and so on. To look at a pedigree and make statements based on percentage of blood, as many people do, is open to all kinds of errors.

Because this aspect confounds many beginners, we will see why this is so. It would seem logical on percentage terms that this would be the case. Let us take one of your females. She inherited 50 percent of her genes from each of her parents.

These create a "new" gene base. Of her 100 percent, she will pass 50 percent to her offspring. But it does not follow that they will be made up of 25 percent each of those she received from her parents. She may pass, based on the random nature of gametes, far more of those received from her sire than those of her dam. The 12.5 percent theory is then blown out of the window. Repeated over a number of generations, it becomes clear that percentage of blood calculations are at best generalities, although they can be a guide. At worst, they can be very misleading.

Based on these comments, you will understand that much beyond the third generation back, the pedigree is of limited value. The gene contribution made by fourth and fifth generation ancestors to the hedgehog you are looking at is very limited indeed.

The only way their contribution could be greater is if they appear a number of times in the pedigree. This would increase the possibility that some of their genes may have reached your hedgehog.

4. The unknown ancestors are as important as the famous ones. Very often, owners and breeders will highlight given outstanding individuals whom they know something about. But they will totally ignore names unfamiliar to them, as though only the former

The male's penis sheath is visible in the middle of the abdomen.

A calm, self-confident hedgehog will likely make a better mother than a nervous one. Since some psychological tendencies are inherited, it also stands to reason that a hedgehog of this type will produce offspring that are easily handled.

are passing on their genes. Those unknown names could have passed on more of their genes than their more famous relatives, as we have just discussed.

Your hedgehog's qualities, or lack of them, are the sum of all of its ancestors' genes, so in trying to determine from whom they came assumes you have information on *all* of its ancestors, not just a few of them. Faults in your stock could as easily have come via famous individuals as via the unknowns in the pedigree, the reverse being true of the stock's virtues. This is where research of a pedigree is valuable, but it is rarely undertaken due to time and cost considerations.

A list of names on a pedigree is virtually worthless unless you know the individuals named. A breeder should always make notes on his own pedigrees of facts that may be useful to him later on.

If you see an individual that is on one of your pedigrees and you notice that it has a rather long snout, write this down on the pedigree. If it has a very large or very small snout, write this down, and so on. In this manner, you will build up a very useful data bank of the individuals on this document.

HEDGEHOG IDENTIFICATION

In order to maintain your records, you will need to apply a system of individual identification to your stock. At this time, there is no NAHA officially recognized system of permanent identification. Ear tagging has been ruled out, while other systems (tattooing, leg banding, and microchip implants) are still under review.

The most used system is to apply colored acrylic or similar water-soluble craft paints. Choose those that are quick drying. In a small herd, you can use blue for males, pink for females. In large herds, you can use any of the extensive range of colors.

GENETICS AND SELECTION: THE KEYS TO SUCCESS

It is important for you as a breeder to understand the basics of genetics if you wish to conduct a successful program. One of the first things you will learn is that genetics is largely based on probabilities—the percentage chance of this or that feature being inherited by a given individual from a given mating when there are variables that can be transmitted.

We can illustrate this in a simple manner once you understand how genes (features) are inherited. Genes are arranged on structures called chromosomes, which are found in pairs in all body cells. The location of each gene on a chromosome is called its locus (plural, loci). At each locus, there is an equivalent gene controlling the same feature on the second chromosome of the pair.

When mating takes place, only one of the paired chromosomes of each parent will be passed to the offspring, thus retaining the

paired situation at each generation. Let's focus on just one gene locus and give it the letter A. We will say it controls good temperament. Its alternative form is a, which produces bad temperament. In reality, temperament is not controlled by a single gene, but by many: it is said to be a polygenic feature. However, here we are using this hypothetically to illustrate one or two points. The genotype of a nice hedgehog will be AA (one A gene on each of the two chromosomes); that of a bad-tempered one will be aa. That of one in between will be Aa. If two AA individuals are mated, the only genes they can pass to their offspring will be A, so all will be AA, thus displaying good temperament. It matters not whether the individuals are unrelated, or brother and sister: what is important is what genes they carry.

If an AA is paired to an aa, the one parent can pass only an A, the other an a, so all of the offspring will be Aa—not as good as one parent, but better than the other. Now, if these Aa offspring are paired to their own type, the mating will be Aa x Aa, and the expectations will be: Aa x Aa = AA Aa aA aa.

There are no other possible permutations. You will note that from two parents with only average temperament, we have now created 25 percent youngsters with super temperament, 50 percent with average temperament, and 25 percent with bad temperament. Let us say those Aa parents were, in fact, brother and sister. They are an example of

A breeding facility should be well thought out and your animals settled in and fully accustomed to their homes before a breeding program is started.

very close inbreeding. Rather than produce poor offspring, they have produced 25 percent that are outstanding—and "purebreeding" for good temperament. They have also produced 25 percent bad individuals.

Clearly, the wise breeder will retain only the AA and Aa offspring for onward breeding, totally rejecting the aa stock. If the AA and Aa are mated, the result will be: AA x Aa = AA Aa AA Aa.

There are now no poor temperaments, and half of the offspring are excellent for this trait. By rejecting the Aa youngsters, you are left with only AA breeding stock. In other words, producing excellent stock is not simply a matter of the genes, but of the breeder's ability to apply selection to the resulting offspring.

If this is missing, as it invariably is with the cash-crazy breeder, then aa individuals are sold to unsuspecting owners. As a

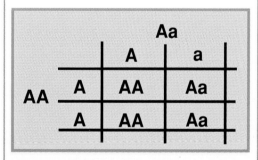

Simple crosses can be calculated by the use of a Punnett square.

result, there will be a steady deterioration in the general standard of temperament in the population as a whole.

As stated earlier, temperament is not so simply transmitted. It is made that much more difficult to evaluate because it is highly influenced by the environment, meaning the way the individual is cared for and handled from an early age. It is a major source of concern for present-day breeders and should always remain so in the future, so it is topical to use in a simple form to show gene actions.

In the foregoing example, the implication of Aa is that it represents a midway sort of blending of the genes. In reality, this is never the case because genes always retain their own identity. Most features of hedgehogs are inherited in a polygenic manner. This means the more of one kind you have for a feature, the more it moves the feature toward the extreme of expression. For example, if 20 gene loci control temperament, and at 16 of them you have genes for good temperament in both parents, then the offspring should display sound temperament, the reverse being as true. Polygenic features thus show gradation from one extreme to another, often (but not always) in a simple additive manner.

It is a case of trying to build up the number of desirable genes while reducing the number of those of undesirable status. This is achieved by selection of stock at each generation. In some colors, such as agouti or albino, they are inherited in a simple major gene manner, and are easy to manipulate and forecast.

In other colors and patterns, they may be determined by the interaction of numerous genes, so they are more complex. But they are still easily calculated once you know the major genes involved in their production, and how these genes are transmitted. Colors can be written down using formulas; polygenic features cannot, because we do not know how many genes are involved.

You will not find books on the genetics of hedgehogs at this time, but this is not important in your study of heredity. Any basic college-level book on genetics will serve your needs.

BREEDING SYSTEMS

Your options with regard to breeding systems are numerous. They are summarized here and should be the source of further study.

1. Inbreeding. This is possibly the most misunderstood breeding method by those who have little or no knowledge of genetics. The reality is that without inbreeding, it would be all but impossible to "fix" desirable qualities into a line of hedgehogs, or any other pet. Just about every hedgehog in the USA is inbred to a greater or lesser degree.

This is easily appreciated when you stop to consider that the original gene pool from which most American hedgehogs were derived comprised no more than a few hundred individuals—at the most. For present-day hedgehogs to be unrelated, given the fact that we are at about the 12th generation, would mean there would have to have been 4,096 unrelated individuals in the original pool. In the case of a 13th generation, the pool would need to have been 8,192 hedgehogs.

Close inbreeding practiced over a number of consecutive generations can produce anomalies, such as breeding depression, susceptibility to illness, reduced size, and other problems. But it can also result in many advantages. However, no sensible breeder would inbreed continually, so at the level likely to be

they are more likely to be in a pure form—homozygous being the correct genetic term.

While many uninformed breeders will shun the word inbreeding, they will quite happily claim that their stock is carefully line bred, clearly oblivious to the fact that this is inbreeding practiced at a more dilute intensity.

It doesn't take a huge area to keep a breeding colony.

seen in these pets, the potential problems of this method are more breeder related than is the system itself.

As we have seen in the genetic example, successful inbreeding is highly dependent on the breeder selecting only the best from litters. If this is not done, any problems in the stock are soon apparent and are magnified because

Unless some degree of inbreeding is undertaken, it becomes impossible to steadily increase the likelihood that certain genes are being fixed into the line while others are being removed. This is why knowledgeable breeders are always very cautious about introducing additional stock to their herds unless they have plenty of information on its likely genetic lineage.

Of course, as you inbreed virtues, you may well do the same to the faults. Indeed, the faults may be genetically linked to the virtues because the latter, under natural conditions, may be healthier if retained in what is called a heterozygous (dissimilar) state or ratio.

By increasing given gene numbers to favor the extreme of a feature, you may increase the recessive genes that create problems to the degree that the problem becomes manifest, which it may not be at a lower level. This is nature's way of protecting the species from undue movement toward extremes of expression that would limit its ability to cope with change.

The objective in a linebreeding program is to increase the homozygous state of the genes within the stock by utilizing given excellent examples a number of times within a number of generations, or using stock carrying those individual's genes. This works very well for independent features but less so when they are negatively linked, as just discussed.

2. Outcrossing. This is the mating of individuals who are unrelated to each other. One or both of a pair may themselves be the product of inbred lines, as long as the members of those lines are not related. This method represents random breeding and has the advantage that it can produce the occasional outstanding individual—rather like the right lottery number that can make you rich. It may also help to avoid some of the problems that "go with the territory" of inbreeding.

However, the down side is that any outstanding individual of this type will rarely prove of any value in a breeding program. Many of the genes that gave it its gorgeous features may be in a heterozygous state. In its litters, the offspring may range from average to very mediocre, depending on the mate used.

When excellent stock is the product of such an individual, this may reflect the quality of the mate rather than of the perceived outstanding individual.

In most animal hobbies, it is not uncommon for a "sparkler" to come along that was produced by this method. The unfortunate result is that breeders clamber to use this individual as a stud, (if it's a male), or obtain its offspring (if it's a female), only to find that these animals produce nothing of merit and may actually undo much that the breeders may have achieved previously in their lines.

On the other hand, an outcross of inbred lineage may have great value to the breeder whose program has come to a standstill because a given fault is so inbred that it cannot be removed by the system. In this case, an outcross may achieve the objective. But this will be true only if it excels in the feature needing improvement, and is sound in all other features. Even then, it may take a few generations before its merits are fully effective.

SELECTION METHODS

The best breeding systems are only as good as the selections made from offspring resulting from them. If you cannot perform this aspect soundly, your program efforts will prove to be wasted. Thought and research into selec-

ICM selection. However, by doing this, they have no records that can be examined at later dates. They may also get carried away by a single good or bad feature that sways their decision of the moment, which might not have been done had they worked against a

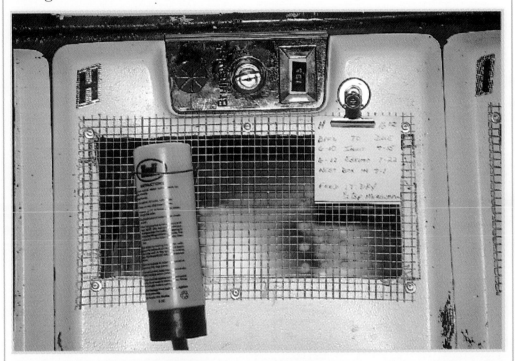

Accurate tracking of breeding and due dates is vital.

tion methods, which are dis-- cussed next, are definitely worth- while for any serious breeder.

Independent Culling Method (ICM): This is a very commonly used method, even if breeders do not know it by this name. Fur- ther, most breeders rarely commit this method to paper, which is unfortunate because they lose out by not doing so. The ICM method is based on selection for multiple features at one and the same time.

Breeders normally rely only on their eyesight to make a simple

selection sheet. So, whatever method you use, *write it down.*

With ICM, you list the features deemed most important in your stock—health, temperament, length, snout length, body shape, color, markings, and so on. You then determine what is to be your minimum acceptance of these features. Any individual that fails to meet *all* minimums will not be retained for future breeding.

With this method, the more features you list, the greater the chance fewer individuals will qualify unless the standards are realistic, rather than too high. You should also be sure that only really important features are assessed.

Comment: ICM will be slow in producing results, but it should result in a steady overall improvement of stock at each generation. It will minimize obvious faults and is a "user friendly" method that has proved itself over the years.

Tandem Selection: With this method, you select the feature that you wish to especially improve. You then find a male that excels in this, and comes from a line of stock which likewise excels. From the subsequent litters, you retain only those displaying the feature to the desired standard. You then select another major feature and concentrate on it.

Comment: This method is useful to make improvements in existing good stock but is less useful where overall improvements are the objective. It is also useful where desired features are genetically linked but less useful where they are in opposition— meaning as one feature improves the other recedes. Generally, it is somewhat limited in scope.

Total Score: With this method, you list the desired features and grade them on a scale of one to ten. You determine the minimum score for onward breeding retention.

Comment: This method is more flexible than ICM because it does

Doing what comes naturally includes looking for a dark hideaway. Under a sofa is a very good choice from a hedgehog's point of view.

A hedgehog enclosure next to the TV and a drafty window is the worst possible combination.

not reject a potentially outstanding individual because it failed in one, or maybe two, features. It is the overall score that is the key. The weakness of this method is that it assumes that all features have equal value—or equal value to you at any given moment, which is rarely the case. Adjusting the feature values, as with marks out of 10, 9, 8, and so on, is not really effective because judgment needs to be based on a constant value.

Total Score and Coefficient: With this method, you utilize total score for consistency of marking (e.g., out of 10), but you multiply it by a variable that reflects the importance of the feature to you. Temperament may be a high priority, so it is given a coefficient of 5. Head shape may be the next priority, so it gets a 4, color 3, length 2, and so on.

Once again, you determine what the minimum score for retention will be. There are two ways to use this method. You may give priority to features that are already sound, whereby the method will then favor them to ensure that they stay that way. Alternatively, you may give needed improvements high priority. Either way, as objectives are achieved, you can alter their coefficient to reflect your changing priorities.

Comment: The method is superior to the others discussed because it will tend to favor retention of stock displaying needed features. It avoids the risk that minor features are given undue credit, yet it allows individuals with faults to be retained if they really excel in a needed feature.

Progeny Testing: With this method, you are able to assess the breeding worth of an individual (usually a male) by evaluating his offspring. This can be done by utilizing the scores from the selection methods already discussed.

If litters from a given sow are assessed after the use of various boars on her, it can reasonably be assumed that those which are best reflect the value of the boar, even if that boar does not appear to be quite as visually impressive as others used on her. He is passing his virtues on. Others may have better visual virtues but are clearly not prepotent for them.

From this brief discussion of selection methods, you will see that there are many roads toward the same objective. The key is, of course, that you apply constant judgment to each individual, that the features selected are chosen with care, and that they are balanced in their importance to your present needs.

In some instances, you may be able to assess a feature when a hedgehog is only a couple of

Begin looking in the nestbox as soon as the female returns from the male's quarters. In this way, she will become accustomed to the movement and light and will be less likely to overreact when you look for newborns.

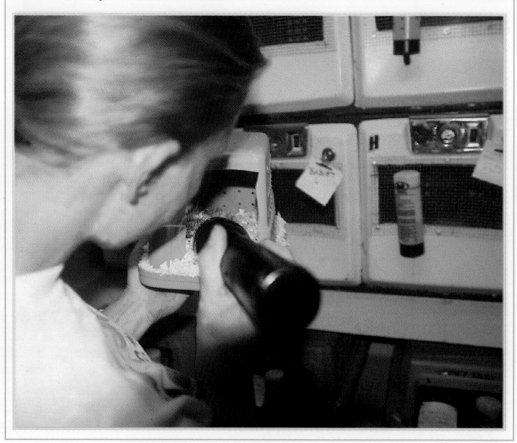

Fresh bedding and good hygiene practices will help to prevent infant mortality related to harmful bacteria levels.

months old; in others, you may have to retain it until it is six months old before a worthwhile evaluation can be made. In this author's experience, if all assessments are made by the eight-to-ten week period, some potentially excellent stock will be sold prematurely.

However, just because a youngster is retained until it is six or more months of age does not mean that you should breed it just because it was retained. It can happen that a promising youngster fails to live up to its early promise.

Likewise, it is also bad policy to retain any stock that fails to look better than their parents, unless they represent the first generation of using an outcross on an inbred line. In this case, it may take further generations before the value of the outcross is evident. For this reason, outcrosses should be used on only a few of your herd until you have had time to see whether the desired objective is being achieved.

Even if you study no further on the topics in this chapter, judicious use of what has been discussed should ensure that your breeding program will be far more successful than if no breeding theory was applied to it.

Stud males should also be checked prior to breeding and should be expected to have the same qualities of handleability and trust that are required of breeding females.

Practical Breeding

Hedgehogs cannot be regarded as especially difficult mammals to breed. This having been said, the offspring can be extremely difficult to rear unless the parents were well chosen, and the rearing conditions are of the required standard. The latter is very important, as many owners have found out at considerable expense.

If you are planning to become a breeder, it is certainly hoped you will have read and digested the various aspects discussed in the previous chapter. If you have become a breeder by chance, as a number of people have because the little pet they purchased was found to be pregnant, you will be more concerned with the practical aspects than theory. This being so, it is hoped that all of the information you need will be found within this text.

GENERAL OBSERVATIONS

Hedgehogs, and most certainly females with newly born babies, are extremely nervous creatures at the best of times. Sows are very protective of their litters. They become more so if contained in a limited area, as many are. A mother with newly born infants will not hesitate to kill and devour them if she feels in any way threatened. She will do likewise if she feels unable, through reasons of diet, to be capable of rearing the infants. These are natural protective and survival instincts.

Some females are extremely good mothers; others are quite the opposite. Mothering instincts are genetic, and in this respect it should not be forgotten that they may have been received as much via the father as from the mother. When problems are encountered, this fact should be considered when trying to trace where poor mothering ability comes from.

Of course, a genetically "good" mother may become a bad one due to the environment. Determining where the problem lies is always difficult in traits that are heavily influenced by the environment (health, parental instincts, temperament, and their like).

Apart from the genetic effect on mothering ability, another effect on it will be that related to domestication, which will improve with passing years as a result of breeder selection. Its ongoing influence will be with respect to physiological changes that will take place within the captive population. Domestication affects a range of characteristics, including parental ability, temperament, the senses, breeding competitiveness, and other aspects. The forebrain decreases (Herre and Rohrs in Grzimek, 1976), and the flow of adrenaline from the endocrine organs is slowed down. As a result, the animal becomes less excitable, less readily stressed, and thus less predisposed to stress and nervous cannibalism

115

or abandonment. The down side is that as this happens, the incidence of reduced fertility (smaller litter size) may result, thus compounding what is already a complex issue.

Reduced fecundity may be attributed to a genetic base, when it may in actuality have been an inevitable consequence of the domestication process, which is intrinsically linked to heredity. Reduced fertility is often a problem within domesticated species. It is not easily overcome, short of an injection of stock from a wild population.

BREEDING FACTS

Sexual Maturity: The African pygmy hedgehog, *Atelerix albiventris*, may become sexually mature when only eight weeks of age. The female may become pregnant at such a tender age—the male normally being rather older before he is capable of actually fertilizing a female, but you cannot count on this. Both sexes have successfully produced litters to known fertile mates at this age (Brodie, 1982). A male weighing only 118g (4 oz.) was reported as being sexually mature (Gregory, 1976).

Suggested Breeding Age: Male or female, especially the latter, are best not bred until they have reached six or more months of age. They are still not, at this time, fully physically mature; but the females are sufficiently so to be able to cope with the stress and trauma of birthing and raising a litter if conditions are conducive to this.

Producing your first litter of hedgehogs requires a lot of planning. Light cycle, temperature, proper weight of the breeding pair, and record keeping are just a few of the essentials.

Females in open wire cages must have the privacy of a nestbox and a very quiet setting.

It is most unfortunate that some of the early breeders in this hobby suggested breeding females at three months of age in order to best capitalize on investment. This was poor advice because, linked with restricted living conditions, lack of selection, and lack of correct diet, it greatly increased the risk of cannibalism, which became and remains a problem in some herds.

When breeding from immature females, the results can be:

1. Stunted development of the female.

2. Smaller and weaker offspring due to the reduced calcium levels of the female.

3. Potentially reduced lactating ability of the female.

4. Increased risk of ill health in the nursing female.

Hedgehogs should be at their proper weight, neither underweight or obese, prior to breeding.

In the case of immature males, there may be a reduced sperm count resulting in smaller (numerically) litter size. The breeding life of this species is not well documented at this time. Unconfirmed reports of hedgehogs having litters well into old age may or may not be typical under optimum condition. As a guide only, it is suggested that not much after four years, it is unlikely that a female will reliably breed and produce healthy vigorous offspring. Males will be capable of breeding until they are quite old, it being litter size and vigor that will decline.

Gestation Period: This is within the range of 34-44 days, the most likely being 35-37. In 50 litters documented by Brodie, 20 percent were born at 35 days, 36 percent in 36 days, and 16 percent in 37 days. Only one litter was produced on the 34th day, and one each in days 41 through 44. The peak range indicated approximates that of this author's stock, and that of most other breeders with whom I have discussed the subject.

Litter Size: In theory, this is one to ten, but a typical litter will be three to six. The survival-to-maturity rate is very variable due to the numerous factors discussed that will influence it. It may be as high as 100 percent under optimum captive conditions. You can work on the basis that if a hoglet survives the first few days, its chances of reaching maturity dramatically increase with each passing day—always assuming that it has a favorable environment. The survival rate will normally be below optimum the larger the litter is beyond the typical range.

Number of Litters Per Year: We should distinguish between how many litters a female is theoretically capable of producing, how many she will reliably produce, and how many are recommended without the risk of physically overtaxing her.

are, frankly, being greedy and giving their females very little opportunity to recover full physical condition between litters.

Weaning Age: An average weaning time will be when the youngsters are four to six weeks of age. However, it must be added that an infant will continue to feed from its mother until it is over three months of age if allowed to do so. It is prudent to allow only

The female is introduced to the male's quarters. A large enclosure is required to accommodate the running and chasing stage of courtship.

With a gestation of 35 days and an average weaning period of the same number of days, the model breeding cycle is therefore 70 days. This gives a potential of 5.2 litters per year. Results would indicate that females will rarely produce more than four litters per year. The safe number is two to three. Those attempting a fourth

females to remain to this age with their mother.

In reality, to remove a youngster of under six weeks from its mother this author regards as poor husbandry practice. It can result in subsequent problems, depending on the environment in which the youngster is placed. At the author's Camelot stud, all females remain with their mother until about eight weeks of age, after which time they move *with* her to an adult female habitat containing other non-breeding females.

At this point, the mother will cease feeding or interacting with the offspring as being her own, whereas she would have continued to do so if left with them in isolation in the breeding quarters.

The minimum age at which a youngster should be allowed to go to a new home is when it is eight weeks old. This is most certainly the case if the hedgehog is going to a pet home rather than to that of an experienced breeder.

Indeed, the prospective pet hedgehog owner, unless circumstances dictate otherwise, is advised to leave the youngster with its breeder until it is about ten to twelve weeks of age. By this time, it is far more able to make a move without the ever-present risk of high stress affecting its state of health.

With the basic breeding facts having been discussed, we can now look at other aspects of practical breeding.

HOUSING

We have already discussed housing, so here only a few additional comments as specifically related to breeding need be made. Once the boar has mated the female, either animal can be removed from the accommodations. Leaving the pair together

Usually, the female appears uninterested while the male pursues her, sniffing and squeaking.

The courtship process often triggers self-anointing behavior.

has little merit. The only effect will be that the boar may pester the female with his unwanted attentions, which are likely to be forcibly resisted. So why take the risk of injury?

The mated female can be retained in her own accommodations or returned to an all-female community if you have one. She will be quite happy leading a normal life up until about a week before she is due to give birth to her litter.

Her breeding quarters are best supplied with *two* nestboxes, assuming the quarters are generous. Providing sufficient space is strongly recommended if you wish to reduce the risk of stress-induced cannibalism. When a

female has very restricted quarters, she becomes hypersensitive to these conditions. It is as though all of her attention is centered on this tiny space—and on her nestbox and babies.

Initially, this will be so anyway, but within a few days, rather than weeks, the female with ample space will soon leave the babies for progressively longer periods. She will reside in her second nestbox whenever she is getting tired of the constant activity and demands of the youngsters—as would be the case in the wild. Like any mother, she needs some time away from her babies if she is not to go insane!

If she is denied this, she may become paranoid over the young-

The female may attack the male during the courtship, but serious damage is rarely done. Biting is normal and may even draw some blood.

sters to the degree that the slightest disturbance is enough to send her "over the edge" and cause her to attack or desert her offspring. While I am sure that poor breeding and selection have influenced the occurrence of cannibalism in hedgehogs, I firmly believe that its basic root cause in some of the early stock was (and remains) created more by the environment than because of any hereditary weakness.

Heredity was the obvious "culprit" for those who were restricting their sows to small cages, rather than for the breeder to seek other plausible reasons for the trait. If the sow has generous housing, she will be more relaxed to start with. This will affect all subsequent events. It is altogether better to avoid problem situations than to have to deal with them once they arise.

BREEDING CONDITION

This term covers all facets of any bred animal from nutrition to fitness, stress state to temperament. In the case of a pet suddenly having an unexpected litter, you are where you are and must deal with the situation almost on a day-to-day basis. The same is not true for a breeder, who should meticulously plan all aspects in preparation for a birthing event. A breeding animal should be in a really fit state, having received ample exercise. If this is not the case, the sow's mothering ability,

PRACTICAL BREEDING

her ability to produce vigorous offspring, and the size of the litter will be adversely affected. If either parent is obese, *do not* use them for breeding until they are slimmer. If you do otherwise, you are courting problems.

The male plays no part in the rearing process. His only role is to transfer sperm to his mate. However, the quantity and potency of his sperm reflect his fitness. The litter size is therefore influenced by the fitness of the male.

If the sow, especially, is not accepting a wide-ranging diet, *do not* breed her until she does so: many problems, including those of cannibalism, are attributable to inadequate diet in the female. Further, the feeding habits of the youngsters will reflect those of their mother.

The NAHA receives many calls from worried owners whose youngsters are refusing most foods offered. This is because these youngsters have been fed on a Spartan diet from birth. A breeder must avoid this situation. The only sure way of doing so is to breed only females that will accept a cosmopolitan diet.

Breed only hedgehogs of solid temperament: If your sow is intractable, *do not* breed her until she can be handled readily. Her aggressive nature may be genetic, but more probably it is environmental. She simply was not handled enough as a youngster. Such acquired traits are not hereditary, but they can be transferred to the offspring early in their lives.

The male's persistent squeaking, sniffing, and pushing finally pay off.

Babies that continually hear, and see, their mother being aggressive are more likely to develop this trait by example than those who, by the same example, see their mother displaying no fear of the owner. This is especially so once youngsters pass the 14-day mark.

If a female is beyond redemption with respect to being tractable, then there can be no justification in perpetuating more of her genes. The same is actually as true of the boar. In his case, he would need to be an outstanding individual, but even then you are gambling that his bad nature is not genetic. Only if the parents are in good breeding condition are they worthy of being bred.

THE CHOICE OF BOAR

All too often, a breeder's choice of a male to cover a given female will be made rather casually. For this reason, we will discuss the subject in depth. Selection is often done a) without due thought for the true value of the male to the line, b) because the male is convenient to use, or c) because the male appears to be a superb specimen. Let us look critically at each of these reasons.

First, however, we should establish a very important point with respect to boars. The male *is* in one sense more important than the female, but very often breeders will raise the status of a male to a level that is totally unjustified. His importance within the hobby derives *not* from the fact that he has any greater influence on the genetic state of the offspring when compared to the female.

Both sexes pass only 50 percent of their genes to the offspring. But the boar, for better or worse, has a greater opportunity to spread his genes through a population at a greater speed than can the female. A sow will, on average, be a dam to only 15 or less babies a year. A good (or bad) boar could sire at least ten times this number without being overworked.

Choosing him should be made only after very careful thought, including his effect locally, meaning within your program, and nationally, as his gene contribution to the population as a whole if he gains notoriety (which will be the case once a show system is in place).

A male used solely because he is convenient, often being owned by the breeder, has no merit. For this reason, breeders should be highly selective of all males they are keeping as studs. At this time in the hobby, most breeders use their own studs, of which they usually have a selection. Now is a good time to really analyze each boar carefully.

If you are just starting as a breeder, look for and use a boar that will be beneficial to your program, not just because there is one two blocks away. If you already own an excellent boar, you are urged *not* to allow it to cover females of other breeders just because you may get a small fee for this service.

Remember, if the female is a mediocre specimen, all those

The choice of a boar must be made carefully, as he has the capacity to spread his genes within a hedgehog population far more quickly than can a female.

terrible offspring will have your boar as their sire. You can imagine what that will do for his reputation. He will be judged by the stock he has in the hobby. Most people are not going to see him. Rather, his worth will be reflected via the offspring he sires. The pedigrees of his offspring will not state that he was outstanding and that the sows were terrible: it will be assumed that poor-quality offspring were as much a reflection of his qualities (or lack of them) as of the dams he covered. Earning a few dollars on stud fees now could cost you many hundreds down the line!

From your perspective, a boar's value should be viewed in one of two ways: 1) What it may achieve in specific areas or traits (such as head structure, temperament, color and so on) and 2) what it might achieve in multiple traits or objectives. The former implies a limited scope, the latter a more long-term view.

There would be little benefit in owning the first mentioned. He should be used but not owned. However, the second may be worth investing in. Bear in mind that there is no merit in using a boar to improve a given feature if the trade-off is that he carries obvious faults in other features.

In choosing either type—and I would be very careful in using the first mentioned—it is not enough that he displays the required feature to the standards needed.

He must be known to pass the feature(s) on. You can establish this fact only by reference to his offspring, which requires some degree of research. This is how top breeders approach the situation. The pedigree is a useful start, but, remember, it is no more than a scrap of paper in the absence of seeing some of the individuals listed on it.

One of the greatest errors that many breeders make is to use a given male for no other reason than that he is well known, or looks magnificent. He usually gains this status because he is a prolific show winner.

A good-looking hedgehog may have gained its looks as much by the chance union of genes as by careful breeding. Winning at a show implies nothing with regard to breeding potential, which is true of many top-winning animals. But breeders continue to flock to shows and use such individuals, thinking that the winners' visible virtues will at a stroke improve their own stock. It rarely happens.

Even when an excellent breeding boar is established, it does not follow that his use will be beneficial to your line. His proportions may be different from those of your stock. His use could completely break up any consistency in your stock and increase its heterozygous state.

In other words, when choosing a boar, select one that has about the same proportions as does your stock. Never attempt compensatory matings—unlike to unlike—on the assumption that they will give you a happy medium. Doing so will merely increase the range of a given feature in your stock, which is not what you want in conformation features. You need an ideal boar in matters of size, weight, and so on, not one that is excessive in them.

On the other hand, when it comes to temperament, color, parental ability, and their like, you need a boar that is far better than average. These are additive features (including color shade) inherited independently, so the more genes you have for them the better.

You can appreciate from this discussion that selecting a boar, at least from a serious breeder's viewpoint, is not as simple as may have been thought. Always remember that when selecting to achieve a singular objective (such as color or temperament), the chances are high that the boar displaying it may be weak in other areas that are sound in your stock.

A great deal of trading off is therefore involved. Sometimes an element of risk must be taken to attain success; at other times, it should be avoided. This is certainly the case where health and temperament are concerned.

THE MATING
You will hear conflicting ideas about mating methods. Some will leave the sow with the boar for a day or two, remove her, and then place her back a few days later. The gap seems inordinately long in some articles that I have read. Others leave the sow with the

Actual copulation may last several minutes and may be repeated several times in the course of one night.

boar for a week. Studies in other animals support the view that a repeat mating within a given time period (usually 12-24 hours) will indeed increase litter size to maximum potential.

This is so in situations where single penetrations are observed (e.g., cattle, horses, dogs, pigs). Hedgehogs, however, mate repeatedly within a given time period. Whether repeat matings after a day or two are beneficial is open to question, assuming the initial matings were effective.

Nonetheless, this author's method is to place the pair together for a couple of days, separate them, and pair them again 12 hours later. If a mating is observed within a few hours of first introductions, the pair are separated and paired again the following day. This, we believe, gives us the best options. Bear in mind that litter size is influenced by genetics, temperature, and the health of the individuals. Genetically, it probably has a low hereditary value (under 20 percent). This means that attempts to select for it by the breeder will generally be a wasted effort. A female producing large litters may

Temperament is an extremely important consideration in the selection of your breeding pair.

not pass this trait to all or any of her offspring, so each female is in that sense an entity unto herself in spite of what some may claim.

The trait is non-additive, which is why breeder selection for it is, at best, speculative. There has been no hedgehog research that I can find on this subject, so the comments are based on data obtained essentially from cattle. This data is used as the guide until specific data suggests otherwise.

If you do attempt to select for litter size, concentrate on the sow because it is she that determines this, though old or highly inbred males can negatively affect this. The male produces enough sperm to fertilize hundreds of babies; it is the number of ova (eggs) produced by the sow that is the all-important factor.

The actual courtship and mating are hectic affairs. The boar will follow or chase the sow around the breeding pen, making soft sounds to impart his desires to her. If she is not ready for mating, she will forcibly reject all his attentions. If things get too violent, it is prudent to remove one of the pair and try the next day.

The very presence of the male induces the sow to release ova into the oviduct for fertilization (induced ovulation). When she is ready, she will stay quite still, spines relatively flat, and allow the mating. There is no prolonged "tie" as in dogs or cats, the actual union taking but a few moments to effect. After a short rest, the process is repeated. Once the female has been penetrated a number of times, she will refuse further attempts by the boar.

Persistence by the male will result only in aggression from the sow.

Whether or not the pair should be left together for a number of days should be based on their compatibility. If, between matings, they appear happy in each other's company, they can be left together; otherwise, part them and try 12 hours later. If the sow is very aggressive at this time, you

PARTURITION (BIRTHING)

When the sow has been mated, you should mark on your calender 35 days to parturition. This will be only an approximation because it is unlikely you will know when her eggs were actually fertilized. Your best guide for determining whether she is pregnant will be by a weight gain, especially during the final ten

Offspring are produced approximately 35 days after breeding.

must assume the first set of matings was successful, so return the pair to their respective quarters.

The final comment on mating is that it is always wise to pair an unproven youngster to a partner that has produced offspring. This removes one element of doubt in the event that no offspring are produced. It also usually results in a more reliable mating.

days of the pregnancy, and by the enlargement and "pinking" of her teats. This is why it is always beneficial to weigh the sow before she is mated.

The ambient temperature should be maintained steadily between 70-75°F. (21-24°C), though it can be raised 2-4°, but this is by no means essential. However, if you do prefer to increase the temperature, do this at

It is not uncommon for the stud's mouth and feet to bleed following breeding—not surprising either!

least seven days before the antici-
pated birthing, and do it slowly.
Sudden heat changes are never
beneficial to animals, especially

provide for the growing fetuses.
On the day of parturition, she
may not leave the nestbox to feed.
This situation is quite normal.

This hoglet is several hours old. The first spines are covered by a skin-like membrane during birth. This membrane dries out in just a few hours, allowing the first spines to emerge.

those about to give birth. Avoid
high temperatures because they
can induce stress in the sow.

Several days before birthing (it
varies individually), sows will start
to shore up the entrance of the
nestbox with shavings. Provide
sufficient bedding material in the
box for her to do this, but not an
excess. If there is too much bedding, the risk of the babies being
buried under it and being abandoned increases.

You will notice a steady increase in the sow's food consumption during the gestation period,
so be sure she gets enough to

The first you will know of the
births is the sound of little
squeals coming from the nestbox.
If you are quiet, and near the pen
during the night, which is when
most births take place, you will
hear a soft cooing sound. This is
the sow actually giving birth to a
little hedgehog.

At birth, the babies are covered
in a membrane. The spines, which
are very soft, lie beneath the
membrane, which shrivels up
within an hour or so. The spines
immediately stiffen on contact
with air. The skin is pink-red, and
the little spines are white. Within

a day or two, the brown of the spines is showing through, assuming the coloration is agouti. At birth, the median spineless tract is very clear, but obvious only on the head as the weeks go by.

From the time of their birth, the babies can crawl around but will normally soon huddle together under their mother to commence feeding. Even at this tender age,

DO NOT DISTURB

Although a female can be handled as normal until about a week before the babies are due, she may become less tractable as parturition approaches. Once the litter is born, a typical female will change dramatically in her attitude, even to owners whom she may normally be gentle with. She will lower her spines, hiss, and charge at any intrusion to her

By 12 to 14 days, a young hedgehog will have spines but no fur.

they are quite tough little critters, because the mother often walks over them and moves them around with her teeth.

Once the litter is born, the mother may venture out for a small meal; but she may not do so for about 24 hours. She will gain nourishment from the afterbirths, which she will consume as each baby is born, and which are rich in nutrients.

nestbox. If you put your hand into the nestbox, she may even bite.

It is therefore best to minimally intrude in her domain. You must, of course, supply her with food and water, as well as tidy up the cage or breeding area. But leave her nestbox well alone during the first week, at the least.

Nest inspection is always a debatable issue. On one hand, if you do not inspect the nest, you

Even before the eyes open, a hoglet will react to strange scents by self-anointing.

Realistically, there is no good reason to handle baby hedgehogs before their eyes open. If the mother were to reject them at this age, it would be difficult to hand rear them.

At 16 to 20 days of age, the eyes begin to open.

The hoglets' survivability increases dramatically after the first fur appears, usually coinciding with the eyes opening.

cannot know whether the babies are in good health or in need of help. On the other hand, by inspecting the nestbox, you may just prompt the mother to attack her offspring. An experienced breeder will know his females and, by trial and error, will have established which he can and cannot take liberties with.

In other words, you can advance your knowledge of female hedgehogs only by taking calculated risks based on many factors. The novice is best counseled not to take chances. You can inspect a nest more easily if the nestbox is constructed so that it has a top-opening inspection door. This way, you can entice the sow out with mealworms, or much favored foods, then have a quick look to count the babies and see that all looks well.

After the first seven days or so, the sow will become less belligerent and less likely to attack her babies if her general environment, and diet, is to her liking. We handle our babies with no problems from as young as a few days old, but it is stressed that we do this only with the utmost care, with only selected sows, and under conditions that the average owner may not have in respect to the size of the accommodations.

After about 10-20 days following the birth, the female will not normally be especially resentful of nestbox inspection. The babies will be crawling around quite well

Self-anointing is triggered by exposure to strange scents and tastes. Most everything is strange to a baby hedgehog at this age, and a lot of time and effort is spent on this odd behavior.

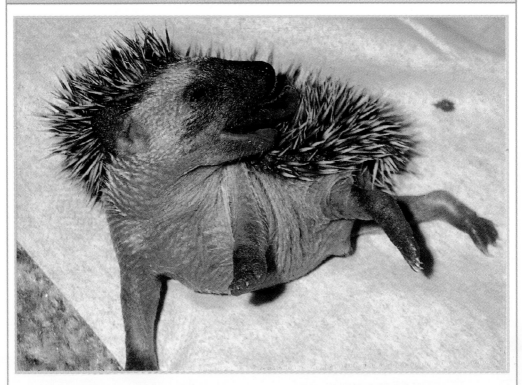

The penis sheath is readily visible on the round, bald belly of this youngster.

Weanling-age hoglets should be marked according to sex and litter when removed from their mother's enclosure.

anyway. By this time, the mother is beginning to spend more time away from the litter. If, after ten days, a mother should attack her babies, this would suggest something radically wrong has taken place in her environment and should be the source of your investigation.

If handling is deemed necessary, use a large clean plastic serving spoon to lift the baby to inspect or move it. Try to avoid direct handling: your scent may elicit fear of nest intrusion in the mother, thus an attack on the youngster. On this matter, a well-handled female may not be as risky as one that is normally not too friendly anyway. The former will be familiar with your scent, so this may not prompt problems.

REARING THE HOGLETS

By the time the babies are 21 days old, they are truly gorgeous little things and, over the next few days, will be emerging from the nestbox to explore. At this age (indeed from the time their eyes open), they should be handled regularly in order to imprint on humans. This is where small herd owners are at an advantage. They can devote more time at this crucial period to the youngsters than can the breeder with many litters to cope with—unless the latter has help.

Handling is now absolutely of prime importance because it will determine whether or not the youngsters will make great pets, or nervous ones, by the time they are ready to go to new homes. You

Non-toxic paints are the standard marking system for hedgehogs.

Open-top housing for weanlings allows observation at feeding time to determine that all are eating well. It also facilitates frequent handling, which is necessary to produce the best pets.

Fortunately, hedgehogs are sturdy animals that usually handle air travel well. If shipped, the shortest, most direct route should be used. Shipping should be avoided during very hot weather or when winter storms could delay arrival.

do not need to spend an eternity with the youngsters. Just a few minutes each day will make an amazing difference—as long as it is each day.

Not all babies "come on" at the same rate with regard to temperament. Some are slow developers, being rather nervous initially, but will make great strides if you persevere with handling and gentleness. Make note of these slow developers because their nervousness is more likely to be genetic than with those that have clearly inherited plenty of genes for being solid. The latter are the ones that should be used for breeding.

FEEDING

Other than what has already been discussed in the feeding chapter, it need only be said that young hedgehogs have healthy appetites. Be sure they are offered a range of foods so that their diet is balanced. This will make it easier for the new owners to care for them. The youngsters will begin eating solid foods when they are about three weeks old. Any food that you give them must be cut up in small pieces because they are unable to cope well with large bits at this age.

If you are especially observant, you may notice that the sow will regurgitate foods for the babies. The babies will prompt her to do this by nudging her muzzle and emitting small squeals. The author first noticed this with a female and babies 26 days old. The mother continued to feed on prompting for a number of days, by which time the babies were coping quite well with solid foods.

Unplanned pregnancies can be prevented by placing a divider in the crate. Any type of tube, nestbox, or hideaway will reduce stress by giving the hedgehog a place in which it can retreat during transport.

This breeding facility offers private nest areas and plenty of room for exercise.

Cannibalism, Abandonment, and Hand Feeding

The first two topics in this chapter are ones that no author enjoys writing about. But the harsh reality when they occur is such that many owners have asked me to include them in this book so that some guidance or explanation is provided.

A female hedgehog may cannibalize or abandon, usually the former, one or all of her litter, depending on its size, for any number of reasons, which are given here. They may give you a clue to the problem(s) you may be (or are) confronted with. You can thus avoid or remedy the situation, as the case may be, in most, if not all, instances.

1. A maiden sow may panic during the birthing process. This is likely to be a higher probability when the female is not yet mature herself. In her fearful state, she may destroy or maim one or more of her offspring. She may also mistake a baby for an afterbirth and likewise destroy it. She may become frightened and abandon the youngsters.

Such a female may have no problems with the second and subsequent babies, or with her second litter. If the second litter is cannibalized or abandoned, she should never be used again for breeding, regardless of her external beauty, assuming the problem is not environmental.

2. A female may attack or abandon a litter if she is in a stressful state. This is easily brought about if there is a lot of noise or disturbance to her environment. This would include interfering children, dogs or cats, loud radios, appliances (vacuum, power tools, washing machine), hammering, lights being turned on and off in an irregular manner, and constant "people traffic" near her cage.

She can also become stressed if the temperature is too hot, excessively humid, or too cold. Limited space will certainly be stressful, and the offspring are soon the focus of the sow's stressed state.

3. A female may devour, maim, or abandon a litter if she is undernourished or being fed a diet that is lacking in certain essential vitamins or minerals. She instinctively knows that she cannot cope, so she does not try to. Often, a sow in this state may abort the litter early in its development, in which case it will never be born. If late in development, a non-resorbed fetus may be expelled, thus dead prenatally.

4. A female that is unwell may destroy her babies, or she simply may be unable to cope, thus abandoning some or all of her babies. She may do likewise if she is suffering from mite or other parasitic infestation. Such para-

sites will create problems for the offspring, quickly making them anemic.

5. An otherwise sound mother may become cannibalistic if the owner, either out of curiosity or a misguided sense of concern for the offspring, constantly interferes with her and the nestbox.

6. A female that lacks calcium may be unable to lactate suffi-

is well cared for and has a previous good record as a mother, if her accommodations are moved just prior to or after parturition. This falls under interference with her environment. Further, hedgehogs that are handled by strangers at about birthing time, or change owners just prior to birthing, are also more likely to react in a negative manner to this situation.

These babies are just hours old. New mothers are very sensitive just prior to and just following birth, and opening the nestbox at this crucial time could trigger cannibalism or abandonment.

ciently; unable to quell the pleas of her babies, she may destroy them.

7. A female may destroy one or more babies because she instinctively senses something is not right with them. You may not be able to perceive a problem, but she may.

8. A female may cannibalize or abandon her offspring, even if she

WHAT TO DO WHEN PROBLEMS ARISE

The first thing you must do when a problem arises is to try and identify the cause. Think carefully of the events that preceded the problem, and that probably prompted the sow's reaction. This done, you must then consider the practical and ethical consequences of any action you take.

One of the more difficult decisions will be whether to intervene or to let nature run its course. This decision is more difficult during the first days after birthing. If a sow has devoured one of her babies, do you try to save the remaining ones, or leave them with the mother? This is a judgment call that requires knowledge of the female, and of all the conditions pertaining at the time the decision must be made. Any advice can be only of a general nature, rather than specific instruction.

The questions you must ask yourself are:

1. Can I assume that if the sow has killed one baby she will do likewise with the others? The answer is "no". She may rear the rest with no problems, especially if an identified environmental problem can be rapidly rectified. But she may not, and that is the great dilemma.

I have been fortunate enough never to have been confronted with cannibalism or abandonment. If I were, and it happened during the first days of a litter's birth, I would let nature run its course, for better or worse. This may seem a harsh reaction, but it is based on the assumption that if there are no environmental or diet problems, it is a case that I have a bad mother, or offspring that she has determined cannot, or should not, be reared.

By taking this stance, the female is given every chance to rear at least one of the young-

sters, and this may be sufficient to induce her maternal instincts if they were temporarily subdued for whatever reason. For myself, it is the more palatable choice of sad options discussed later, assuming hand rearing or fostering was not one of them.

There is no gain to the hobby as a whole in attempting to save every youngster simply because it was born. By doing so, you remove any substitute for natural selection that would allow only the fittest and, it must be added, luckiest to survive.

The minute you become a breeder, you take on the onerous responsibility of replacing nature in deciding which offspring will and will not be allowed to survive if things go wrong. As you know, nature in the wild can be very cruel at times. If every youngster born were to survive, this would create enormous problems to its species, and to all others within its ecosystem.

If an offspring was especially rare, there would be greater justification in attempting to save it. But when this situation does not prevail, the saving of a baby that might prove to be a poor parent itself, or have other problems, has no merit other than that of compassion. This merely passes on the problem to others. It potentially increases the likelihood that the problem will get worse in the population as a whole.

You cannot talk of breeding excellent stock for parenthood, vigor, and their like, if you are going to try to save every individual that nature had determined should not survive. Further, in this example, the mother would never be used again for breeding. I would not take a chance that her problem was not genetic.

2. If I intervene at this early age, what are my options? If you have another female with a litter of the same age, there is the possibility that she may foster the surviving youngsters. Your other option is to hand feed the babies,

It would take a rare combination of talent, persistence, and luck to successfully hand rear a newborn infant. Fostering to another new mother is risky but more likely to succeed at this stage.

If a litter was abandoned, or attacked by the mother, after its first week of life, I would be more inclined to try and save the youngsters on the grounds that something must have happened to prompt the female to suddenly do an about-face in her attitude to her offspring. During that first week, the youngsters would have received a goodly supply of colostrum via the mother's milk. This would improve the chance of the babies staying healthy during the hand-rearing period.

or have someone else do this for you.

If this is attempted, you must first understand that it will consume substantial amounts of your time. Do you have the time necessary for such an endeavor? If not, there is no point in trying to save the baby only to cause its death by what would amount to neglect. Even if you do attempt hand rearing, one or more of the babies may still die.

Having considered the ethical problems, we can now look at

practical solutions in attempting to save offspring, or in how best to terminate their short lives.

ENVIRONMENTAL PROBLEMS

Lack of privacy and space are recurring problems with pet owners. The answer is that if the sow has killed a baby, she must be removed to a quiet area where there will be minimal disturbance to her quarters. At the same time, if she is confined to a small cage, she must be given more space so that she does not feel trapped.

It may be argued that most breeders maintain their stock in cages, but they are in a controlled environment where children, dogs, and all of the many other noises and disturbances are not going on around them, and especially when babies are being born. But breeders, too, have to make decisions when things go wrong.

When a pet owner is presented with a litter not planned, the female was probably too young and should never have been allowed to be mated. She has not come from a settled environment—the very fact that she has presented the owner with a litter indicates her unsatisfactory immediate background.

If the mother has cannibalized one or more newly born babies and you fear for the others, yet you know you cannot hope to hand rear or foster them, the kindest course of action would be to have your vet induce euthanasia if you do not want to let nature run its course. In the event that you just cannot get to a vet, and the babies are newly born,

the most humane method open to you for euthanasia is placing them into a cold environment, which they will succumb to quite quickly.

No one likes these options, but I'm afraid there is no magic formula: you are being presented with the hard realities that life sometimes forces upon us. It is for this reason that I would let nature run its course because, hand rearing or fostering apart, it is the only option that might give each youngster a chance to survive if the sow suddenly decides to care for the remaining babies.

Thereafter, she may prove to be an excellent mother. You will never know that if you have taken that chance away from her, and from the babies. Pat Storer (1994) has had success with removing newly born babies from their mother when cannibalism was evident. They were returned to the mother (one at a time) 24 hours or so later. By this time, their small spines are growing. Pat has found the mother far less likely to attack such babies. In the interim period, you must hand feed them.

If the problem is one of inadequate diet, then, while you can try and remedy this instantly, the chances of it having an immediate effect are slim at best. But they are worth trying. Do understand that in the wild, the undernourished female's instincts are for self preservation. It serves no survival purpose for her to be unable to feed her offspring, and risk dying herself, if she can abandon or consume the babies and in so doing increase the chances that she will survive to rear litters when times are better.

ABANDONMENT

There is less occurrence of abandonment than cannibalism based on the telephone calls and letters received by the NAHA from concerned owners. Some of the reports of abandonment are not it is a case that the babies start to crawl at birth. If they are not in a closely confined area, they wander almost aimlessly seeking their mother, and the mother cannot keep them together.

If the substrate is of deep shavings, they can become buried and therefore out of sight. The female will attempt to gather up her

The risks of cannibalism or abandonment are greatest during the first ten days. By the time the babies are fully spined, the mother has usually settled into the routine of motherhood, and only lack of food or a terrible upset would cause problems.

actually this at all. You must determine whether this is the case, or whether it is simply a matter of the sow having misplaced a youngster. This is scattering rather than abandonment.

What may happen is this. If the female is not happy with her nestbox, she will give birth to her babies outside of the box. She will move about somewhat, but mostly youngsters; but unless she can keep them in a given confined space, they will soon be crawling around again. Eventually, she may settle for keeping just two or three around her, taking less care of the others. These start to lag behind the rest and may die, or she may cannibalize them.

Abandonment occurs when the mother refuses to gather or nurse the babies, yet may not go as far as to cannibalize them. She simply moves away whenever one gets near her. She may nip it or even throw it outside of the nestbox that she is using. Of course, the babies will not survive for very long if this is the situation.

Such a problem is more readily overcome than abandonment. First, try to establish whether the youngsters have crawled out of the nestbox—are others still in it? In this case, use a plastic spoon to scoop them up and gently place them back into their nest. At the same time, if there is a sparse amount of shavings at the nestbox entrance, add more. This should be done by the person whose scent the female is most familiar with. If any youngsters still crawl out, try placing a clean piece of flat granite or another similar piece of rock in front of the nestbox so that the babies cannot get out, but leaving sufficient space for the mother to clamber over it so that she can feed and drink. A strip of wood will effect the same end.

If the mother has not used the nestbox and has scattered the litter, you must offer her an alternative. You can use a plastic trash can (turned on its side) that is secured by rocks at the entrance. Using a long-handled spoon, place the babies into the back of the can. Next, place the mother at the entrance, and see how things go.

If she brings the babies out, you must offer her another choice until you supply one to her liking.

This can be a real test of your patience. But it will work if this, rather than something else in the environment, is the problem.

If the female has abandoned the babies, the usual cause of her problem is fear of the youngsters, or stress, so the condition is most likely to occur with first-time mothers. However, the problem could be related to the environment. You should double check that parasites in the nestbox, and on her, are not also a factor. This means handling her, but you have little option in this instance.

It is always possible that a mother will abandon one or two of the babies for her own reasons, yet accept the rest. It may be that someone has handled a baby and left on it an unfamiliar scent. It may be the case that she has limited milk, or that she senses the baby has a problem. In all of these instances, you are back with the decisions already discussed.

In these situations, it may be worthwhile to move her housing to another location, or to try and provide her with more spacious housing. Basically, as with cannibalism, you have nothing to lose by trying this because whatever is to be attempted must be done rapidly.

SHOULD YOU MOVE THE YOUNGSTERS?

Hedgehogs that are given the opportunity to roam freely in a home may move their offspring from one site to another, rather as cats will. The author's experience of this may help to prevent a potential danger of cannibalism. Our first hedgehog, Tiggywinkle, lived in a cage in our home. She gave birth to six lovely babies. As was normal, she left her cage every evening to feed and wander around the dining room before returning to her babies.

When the babies were about six days old, builders started to work outside of the room using drills, saws, hammers, and so on. On the third night, I noticed Tiggy carrying what I thought was a tiny mouse! She took it into the living room and placed it behind a book unit. Upon inspecting the nest, four babies were missing. As I searched for them, Tiggy appeared with number five and placed it under a sofa.

I was satisfied that she would not be bothered by my scent, so I took the others back as I found them; but she quickly mouthed one at a time and off she went to relocate them. Eventually, five were placed back in the nest. I lifted Tiggy, complete with baby six in her mouth, and placed her back in the cage and closed the door.

Her reaction was to take another baby and start pacing at the cage bars. The poor baby was being knocked from one side to the other each time she turned around. I feared for its life. I took the baby from her, placed it back in the nest, and offered her some tasty mealworms—but to not avail. She simply gathered another baby and started the pacing again.

It was the middle of the night. Something drastic had to be done before the builder arrived the next day. I took her and the babies to the hay barn, filled a very large multi-horse feeder with shavings, rocks, logs, and the nestbox complete with Tiggy and the babies. She emerged with one and immediately began clambering over the rocks and logs with the poor youngster dangling from her mouth. It was dropped many times as she traveled around the feeder.

Next, I prepared an office trash can, which was larger than her nestbox, and placed the babies and Tiggy into it. No good...Seconds later out she came with another baby, and off she went banging and dragging it around her new, large home. I added more rocks to the nestbox entrance and a log tunnel. I took the baby from her and placed it with the others well into the back of the can. Then I put Tiggy into the can.

About two minutes elapsed before she came out again—to my great relief with no baby! She explored her new environment before returning on hearing the squealing youngsters. The next day I carefully checked in case the trauma had prompted cannibalism. She lay there on her side with all six babies feeding happily, and there were no further problems.

The event, and Tiggy, taught me a great deal about hedgehogs. It highlighted just how important space is in reducing stress, and what could have happened had she been forced to remain in the cage in that state. The daily pre-

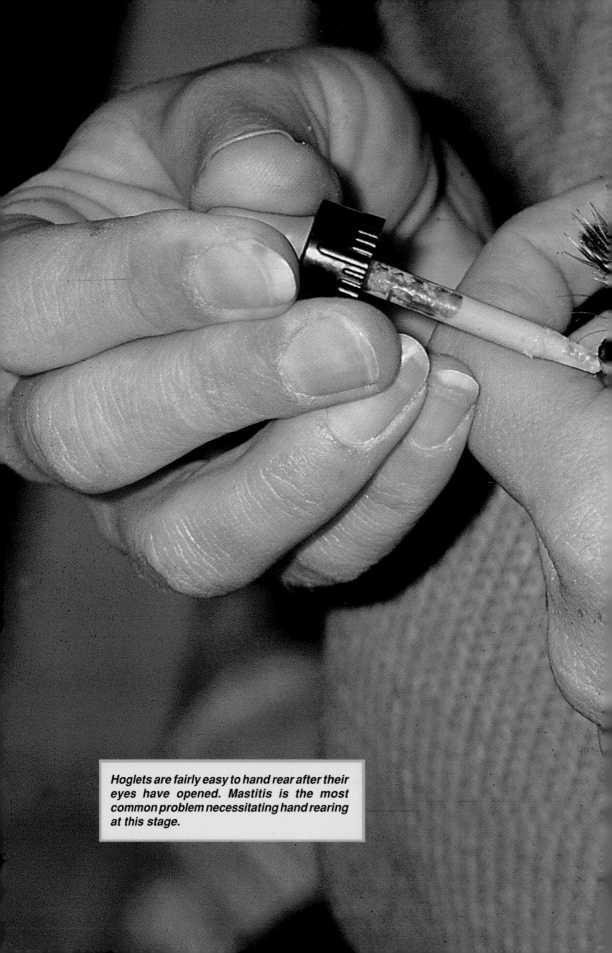

Hoglets are fairly easy to hand rear after their eyes have opened. Mastitis is the most common problem necessitating hand rearing at this stage.

birthing freedom that she enjoyed took her into parturition as a very mentally balanced female. It carried her through those first days without attacking her babies. It allowed her to let me handle such young offspring when she was in an obviously agitated frame of mind.

Sometimes, when you are faced with a major problem, you must take calculated gambles on the outcome. But if you try to place yourself in the mind of your female, you can often overcome the dangers by giving her what she may be wanting, and cannot get if she feels threatened or imprisoned. Remove the tension, and you just may remove the problem.

FOSTERING

Good mothering hedgehogs will usually accept the babies of other sows in many instances. The age of the orphans is not so much the major factor: it is the nature of the mother that will determine success. Some breeders always have matings arranged so that two females will have litters of almost the same age. The advantage of fostering is that it provides an insurance against the possibility of a female dying while her babies are still nursing, or in order to relieve her of some burden if she has a large litter, while another female has a small one.

The disadvantage of fostering is that if it is used solely because a given female has a bad mothering record, it offers no advantage to a breeding program, or to the hedgehog population as a whole.

It merely perpetuates poor parental genes via the fostered offspring.

The potential effect of this can be seen in domestic Gouldian finches, and some other foreign birds. In this species, it resulted in a situation in which it was the norm, rather than the exception, to foster chicks to Bengalese or Zebra finches because of poor parental ability.

Breeders of valuable birds also use this method, as well as incubators and hand rearing, to increase the total offspring per year. When a female is deprived of her chicks, she will have another round of eggs more rapidly than would be normal. Nor is she subject to the physical strain of rearing the offspring.

When an animal breeder has a very fine individual, but one that proves to be a bad mother, there is the obvious temptation to foster her offspring to a lesser female who is a good mother. It is hoped that you will never foster for these various commercial or self-interest reasons. The long-term effect of such a policy can only be deleterious to the hobby.

So, assuming your need is based on that first discussed, you should proceed as follows. Try to entice the proposed foster mother out of her nestbox with some delicacy. While she is out, place the abandoned baby into her nest, preferably well in among the other babies. Then wait and watch what happens. Do not handle this baby. Instead, use a plastic spoon, unless you are very sure that the mother will not react to your scent on the youngster.

If the baby is attacked, I'm afraid that is that; but if it is only rejected, try placing the youngster just inside the nestbox entrance. Its crawling and squealing (depending on its age) may encourage the sow to gather it up and place it with the rest. If she simply throws it out of the nest again, you must either try another female, or resort to hand feeding.

Before you attempt to foster, you might place a small identification mark on the baby so that you can identify it later and monitor its progress. (This is not necessary if the hedgehog's coloration is different from the rest of the litter.) Be sure the paint is thoroughly dry before handling the animal. Marking this baby can be beneficial in helping fostering, but it can also be the opposite. As with all attempts to change the course of nature, there are inherent risks to be weighed against the potential benefits of success.

Some breeders will smear some of the mother's soiled litter onto the fostered youngster. This author has never been convinced that any female animal is so easily fooled! But it is always worth trying.

Finally, it is possible that another animal species may accept orphaned hedgehogs. The choice, perhaps surprisingly as it is a natural enemy, is a tame rat. The risks of using such a mother are no more than with a foster hedgehog—but a nursing rat with babies may be easier to locate in your area. She may kill the youngster, throw it out of her nest, or move all of her babies as

cited by Kranz (1995).

She may denude it of its quills, or she may prove to be an excellent mom, though I have not heard of success as yet using these rodents. The hoglet would need to be only a day or two of age to minimize the risk that she regarded it as food rather than as an infant in need of nursing.

HAND REARING

Hand rearing animals, especially parrots, has been developed into a fine art where "imprinted on human" pets are required. The resulting youngsters invariably become extremely tame and confiding. However, at this time, the procedure in hedgehogs is still in its infancy. Be aware that the success rate may be nothing near 100 percent unless attention to detail, and the ambient conditions, are almost ideal. Depending on the age of the orphan, you will need to be feeding the youngster every few hours 24 hours a day.

HOUSING

The essential requirements are that the "orphanage" is draft free, can be readily sterilized, and its temperature can be controlled. A small aquarium meets these needs. It will, ideally, be large enough to feature a nestbox so that the orphan is not subjected to any intense lighting. It will be located in a warm room, in a shaded area not exposed to direct sunlight.

The nestbox can be lined with shavings, but there is no necessity to line the rest of the housing.

The infant will not be venturing out until it is about three or more weeks of age. A lip on the front of the nestbox will prevent its crawling out.

TEMPERATURE

The ambient room temperature should be maintained at about 72-80°F (22-27°C). It is better not to use a "white light" lamp to provide local heat because of its light intensity. However, a colored (orange, red, blue) spot, or tungsten bulb of about 75 watts, will work fine. You must suspend the lighting unit above the nestbox so that the air temperature at the nestbox roof will not exceed 80°F; otherwise, the inside box temperature may get too hot and stress the orphan.

The inside nestbox temperature should be about 85°F, which would equate the situation when the mother and her babies are all huddled together. But, while general protocol can be given, always remember that each baby is an individual. Observe if the orphan seems content, lethargic, or too active and squealing. Once they are a few days old, and if too active, you might reduce the temperature a degree or two. The reverse is needed if they are lethargic.

An alternate heat source would be a heat pad or cable (the latter from your local aquarist store if you are using an aquarium) under the housing. Regulate by a thermostat. You should try to obtain a clinical maximum/minimum thermometer so that you can check the temperature each day inside the nestbox, but any thermometer is better than nothing.

IMPLEMENTS NEEDED FOR HAND FEEDING

Two factors are vital when hand feeding any animal. The first is that the implements must be sterilized before and after each use. This can be done using commercial baby bottle solutions, or simply holding the feeder in the steam of a boiling kettle. The latter just before use is beneficial, even if a solution has been used.

The second factor is that the food must be offered at about hedgehog body temperature (mean 95°F/35°C). If the food is too hot, this will induce the youngster to be more reluctant at subsequent feeds; if it is too cold, this could create digestive upsets, which are often fatal when they happen in very young orphans. The feeder must also be warmed, never hot nor cold; otherwise the baby will reject it. If a number of babies are hand fed, do not forget to reheat the milk/food to the required temperature for each baby.

As for the actual implements, you can choose from a variety of them. They include an eye-dropper, a short length of small-diameter rubber tubing over a syringe, a catheter cut to about 2.5cm (1 in.) on a syringe, a dental irrigation syringe, even a spoon. Tube feeding is not recommended due to the inherent risk of the liquid entering the respiratory tract and flooding the lungs.

When using syringes, you must guard against the possibility of releasing the milk/food too quickly. This can cause gulping, with the risk of taking in too much, as well as air, with resulting choking and, again, the passage of the liquid into the air tract. If using a spoon, it can be difficult to assess quantity taken due to the amount of spillage.

COMPOSITION OF MILK

Even in human females and cows, probably the two most researched animals, the exact composition of milk is still not completely known. The situation in hedgehogs is well down the list, so there is a high element of chance in whatever formula is used. The problem is that breast milk is not consistent in its content, but changes as feeding progresses.

For example, fat content changes: usually it increases, with resulting decreases in other constituents, such as lactose and proteins. The time of day when the feed is given also alters the fat content, and it has been established in humans that the composition of the milk at one breast is not always the same as that at the other. Information in hedgehogs is therefore pragmatic, rather than established via scientific research.

With this stated, it has been found that cow's milk contains too many fat particles of an undigestible type that creates problems in hedgehogs. Esbilac, a commercial milk replacer, is based on skimmed cow's milk to which egg yolk, minerals, and vitamins have been added. It is perhaps the most popular choice in the USA, Great Britain, and mainland Europe.

Other alternatives are kitten milk replacer (KMR), which has a closer fat content to hedgehog milk than does Esbilac, but a greater differential in its protein content. Both have a lower water content (71 percent) than that of hedgehog milk (79 percent), based on data quoted by Storer (1994).

In the absence of these two products, your next choice would be goat's milk, to which egg yolk and vitamins are added. Sheep's milk is better than cow's milk, but less readily obtained by the average owner. If cow's milk is the only option, use low fat skimmed, again adding egg yolk and a vitamin supplement.

FEEDING SCHEDULE

Before giving you a schedule of feeding, it must be emphasized that what a baby will consume, and what is good for it, are not the same. With this in mind, it is infinitely better to feed a very young orphan small amounts and more often. This reduces the risk that undigested foods will remain in the digestive tract to ferment and create gastro-intestinal related problems, which may prove fatal.

You must also encourage defecation by gently stoking the abdominal-urogenital region of the baby after each meal. You can use a cotton swab or your cleaned finger to effect this. It is very helpful if you have accurate scales so that you can weigh the baby before and after feeding.

This will give you a good idea of food intake (assuming the baby has not defecated after feeding and before being weighed). A youngster should make a steady daily weight gain. A drop in weight could indicate the first signs of a problem.

Birth–3 days: Feed every 2-3 hours throughout the day and night, giving 0.5–1.5ml of milk. Be sure to clean the baby's face after each feed, and stimulate bowel movements.

4–8 days: Continue feeding every 3 hours, but increase the quantity, as the baby will be getting larger. It may consume about 2–4ml, depending on its size.

9–14 days: During this period, depending on how the baby looks and takes its feeds, you can feed every 4 hours. You can now have a six-hour break during the night because in the wild the mother would be away hunting at this time. Beware of the baby overfeeding. Check that its urogenital area is not becoming swollen if it starts to refuse its feed. It needs to expel fecal matter to prevent problems.

15–21 days: The gap between meals can be increased to 3–4 hours and the quantity increased. At this age, a healthy robust baby will be taking 2–5ml at a feed. During the latter days of the period, try adding a little baby food (chicken, meat) to the feed.

22–30 days: During this period, you can increase the baby food content. See if the youngster will lap from a shallow saucer. By now the baby will probably come to you as soon as it is feed time, and it will be defecating without the need for stimulation. But continue to do this with slow developers.

31–40 days: You can increase the baby food content and try offering tiny morsels of meat, chicken, and mealworms. You might add pureed apple and banana to the milk feed. You can reduce the number of feeds to every 5 hours, extending this at night to 7 hours. Start reducing the milk content toward the end of this period.

41–48 days: The youngster should by now be eating solid foods, and you should continue cutting back on the milk content, especially if it is lapping water. It may not be able to cope well at this age with hard cat biscuits. These can be moistened in gravy stock, or warm water, and allowed to stand for a few minutes before being fed. This way, they swell before, rather than after, the youngster digests them.

During the early weeks of hand feeding, you might try adding to the feed a tablet that aids in the digestion of milk. Kirsten Kranz (1995) found this to be beneficial in helping overcome digestive upsets.

DEHYDRATION AND OVERHYDRATION

To conclude hand feeding, mention should be made of two conditions that are not infrequently met in rearing very young mammals. Dehydration is a loss of water greater than the intake volume. Overhydration is the retention of water such that it changes the osmotic pressure between cells and extra cellular space. Both conditions represent abnormal total water balance situations and can rapidly result in death. This is especially so with babies, whose total water composition will be on the order of 75 percent of total body weight.

Unfortunately, the chemistry of water balance is very complex. With very young hedgehogs, you do not have the possibility of diagnosing the source of the condition, only that it exists. This can be detected if the skin loses its elasticity, the eyes become sunken, involuntary muscle twitching is seen, and if the youngster feels cold to the touch.

If an infant refuses its milk, it becomes imperative that it receives water in the form of fluid replacers, or water to which dextrose or glucose has been added. If these are not accepted orally, you must ask your vet to supply the fluid via a stomach tube. Administration subcutaneously is the next potential route if the condition is not very advanced.

In the case of advanced dehydration, intravenous administration, with the attendant risk of overload, must be resorted to. In a young hedgehog, the danger of shock-related side effects of injections are such that a lesser-of-two-evils situation is evident. The risk of procedure choice must be assessed based on the condition, age, and tractable state of the individual. But, one way or the other, body fluid content must be maintained while adjustments to the milk feed are considered in order to create greater acceptance.

In spite of the risk of failure, and subsequent heartache for you if this happens, the pleasure derived from successful hand rearing will be tremendously gratifying in the lovable youngster that can result from your devoted efforts.

Be prepared to lose your heart (and many nights' sleep) to the orphans that you bottle raise.

Health

The hedgehog's dramatic rise in popularity as a new exotic pet is not without its problems from a health care and treatment standpoint—especially the latter. Many vets have been caught "off guard" by this little animal for a number of reasons. It is an insectivore, the first species from this order of animals that most vets will have encountered, unless they have experience in zoological institutions.

Little data on physiological values, pathogens, treatment and its known efficacy are available to the average vet at the time of writing. Information can of course only come via study and practical experience at treating problems as they arise. The result of this is that because of the dearth of information, some vets have preferred not to treat hedgehogs.

By the time of this text's publication, it is hoped that the situation will have improved dramatically as a direct result of the growing number of hedgehogs that vets will be confronted with, and from which they will gain experience.

The problem is made no easier due to the fact that hedgehogs are not always the most willing of patients. Their penchant to curl into a tight ball unless well socialized makes clinical examination rather a prickly affair in many instances, certainly more so than is the case with most other pet patients. Sedation of especially intractable individuals may be required in order to conduct a thorough examination.

The reality of this health preamble underscores two important aspects of present hedgehog husbandry. The first is that the old adage of "an ounce of prevention is better than a pound of cure" is especially true. The second is that the actual advice on diagnosing and treating problems is limited and based on what little has been established to this point in time.

AVOIDING PROBLEMS

In order to avoid problems, you must first understand how they develop, how they proliferate, their effect on your pet, and finally how they can be eradicated. You must also be able to tell when your pet is showing signs of ill health, and what sort of information your vet will appreciate once you are satisfied the hedgehog is in need of treatment, or at the least an examination.

HOW PROBLEMS START

Your hedgehog's health is determined by many factors, any of which can be the precursor of minor or major problems. Sometimes an insignificant problem, such as a cut, can give rise to secondary bacterial or fungal infection. This can then become a major problem. A slight chill left unattended can develop into pneumonia. It could also give rise to other respiratory problems.

These in turn have the effect of reducing the pet's ability to fight off other pathogens (disease-causing organisms). Low housing temperature will create a situation in which the hedgehog's immune system is slowed down, making the pet more vulnerable to bacteria. Excess heat will stress the animal, as well as an already sound diet, can result in hypervitaminosis, which can lead to numerous health problems.

Lack of hygiene is of course a major source of infection. It provides the kind of conditions in which pathogens can rapidly multiply. Further, it then enables them direct access to

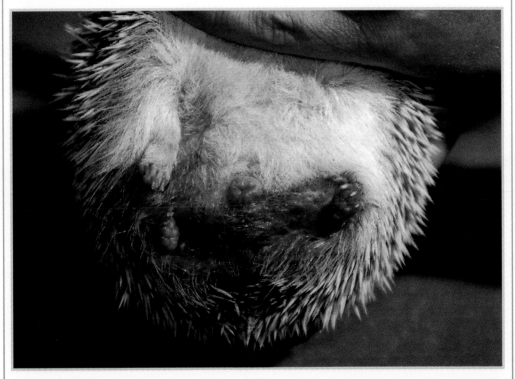

This male hedgehog is showing both diarrhea and a rash, definitely time for a visit to the veterinarian.

increase the rate at which microscopic pathogens will reproduce. It will also increase the rate at which soft foods (fresh meat, mealworms, canned food) will go sour and attract flies and other insects. An inadequate diet results in a debilitated individual that has a reduced immune system, so it is wide open to all kinds of pathogenic attacks. Excess vitamins, supplemental to their host—your pet—either via the food, the shavings, the water, or direct inhalation/digestion by the hedgehog as it forages around and eats.

The problem may not have started in your home, but in the seller's premises. Alternatively, it may have arrived on the clothes of a visitor, via another pet in your home, or from pets kept under unsanitary conditions that live near your home. Pathogenic eggs/spores can travel vast distances on the wind and settle anywhere conditions are favorable to their being able to survive and multiply. Such conditions include rotting vegetation in your garden, trash left to attract flies, and so on.

Problems can also come via seemingly innocuous routes. For example, you may handle your pet after having spent time gardening. Many parasites and their eggs live in garden soil. They are easily transported to pets. This is especially a problem when you live in a heavily populated area in which thousands of pets are being kept in relatively close proximity to your own.

A problem may have started via a young hedgehog's mother. If she is infested with worms before the baby is born, those worms will be present in the unborn fetus. Any problem that she has can be transmitted to unborn offspring. Further, certain illnesses may be genetic, in which case treatment may be difficult, or not possible. In other instances, the genetic influence may be to reduce the ability of the hedgehog to cope with problems that other individuals would have no difficulty with.

Very often, pet owners seek a simple answer to both the problem, its source, and the cure. It is hoped that the foregoing will illustrate that problems are rarely simple, nor are many diseases the result of a single causal agent. Invariably, a number of problems are happening at one and the same time, and their combined effect shows itself as a condition such as diarrhea, respiratory problems, and their like.

PATHOGENS

These disease organisms are ever present. You cannot eradicate them forever with a sudden burst of hygiene, the use of sprays, disinfectants, and their like. As fast as you kill them, they will return if you are providing the sort of conditions that are favorable to their multiplication.

It is a case that good husbandry techniques must be such as to continually minimize the opportunity for proliferation of organisms—both seen and unseen. The latter are the most difficult to control simply because you cannot see them.

Once a pathogen or parasite has found a host, its sole object, as with any other organism, is to survive, feed, and multiply. This it does on the flesh and blood, thus bodily cells, of your hedgehog. Once established, it destroys the cells it lives in, multiplies by simple division, and progresses to adjacent cells. Ultimately, its effect is to disrupt normal body metabolism to the degree that it no longer functions correctly. Foods cannot be fully absorbed, organs become less efficient, and the whole process of breakdown increases.

To counter this, the immune system tries to isolate the pathogens. To help the situation, basic body rhythms slow down so that no excess energy is wasted. All resources are eventually directed at the source of the problem. The animal becomes listless. It shows disinterest in food, needed energy being acquired by oxidization of existing tissue (fat, then muscle).

The eventual outcome will be the death of the animal if it is forced to continue living under conditions that favor the survival of the pathogens more than they do the survival of the hedgehog. It vented from becoming complete is if you interrupt the life cycle of the growing pathogenic population. This can be done via hygiene, via changing or moving the site of the accommodations, by improved feeding, and of course by obtaining veterinary advice and treatment.

However, vet treatment is at best a short-term expediency that

Frequent inspection of the hedgehog, from nose to tail, will alert you to problems before they become life threatening.

is that simple. Even before the host is very ill or dead, further colonies will establish themselves in other healthy tissue—such as other pets. By this means, disease is able to spread from one animal to another, ultimately to the entire available population (as with a breeder's herd).

The only possible way the vicious cycle of disease arrival, attack, and spread can be pre- buys you time in which to correct any underlying problems. If this is not done, then history will simply repeat itself. There is a tendency to expect too much from a vet, especially when matters are left to the point where the vet is up against an almost impossible situation of having little or no time in which to diagnose the problem. You cannot treat a pet until an accurate diagnosis is available.

When diagnosis is not established, the best that can be done is for the vet to take into account all conditions, then make a calculated guess based on experience and knowledge of pathogens, drugs, and their efficacy record. The current problem is that drugs proven safe and effective for hedgehogs are by no means established and agreed upon, even by hedgehog experts.

IS YOUR HEDGEHOG ILL?

Deciding whether your hedgehog is ill can be determined via two routes. One will be any clinical signs of ill health; the other will be by behaviorial changes. As the latter often precedes the former, we will discuss them first. Additionally, behavioral changes may be the only signs you will be given of a potential illness.

With this in mind, it follows that unless you devote some time to interacting with your pet, you will hardly notice any such changes. Because the less-than-tractable hedgehog is likely to curl into a ball at your approach, it is an especially difficult pet to observe when it has a problem. This underscores the importance of obtaining only a very well socialized pet.

BEHAVIORAL INDICATORS OF ILL HEALTH

One of the problems in assessing behavioral changes as part of health diagnosis is that related to temperature and estivation. Normally, when an animal becomes lethargic and sleeps for longer periods, this suggests something is amiss. Not necessarily so with a hedgehog, which may be in torpor, depending on the temperature. If the pet has been active and then becomes much less so, even though there has been no drop in its ambient temperature, you can suspect that it may not be well. However, if you have only recently acquired the hedgehog and it becomes lethargic, you should raise the room temperature a few degrees and see if this results in greater activity. If it does, it is probable that it was previously accustomed to a somewhat higher heat level, which accounted for its lower activity level when you first obtained it.

If it is a friendly little pet, but then starts to hide away when it would normally be active, this is suggestive of a problem. Likewise, the friendly pet that suddenly displays reluctance to be handled may do so because this is causing it pain.

If the hedgehog displays little interest in its food or water, this is not normal for these animals, which should have healthy appetites once settled into your home. However, appetite may fall back a little if the temperature gets too hot—but water intake will not: indeed it may rise somewhat. Hedgehogs do scratch themselves periodically, but excessive scratching is not normal and indicates parasites.

CLINICAL SIGNS OF ILL HEALTH

In order to be able to observe physical signs of ill health, it is essential that you handle your hedgehog every day, and that you observe it while it is feeding. If you have obtained a pet that seems to stay in a ball every time you approach, which indicates that you obtained the pet before finding out about hedgehogs, you must not give up on it. *Only* by daily gentle handling can it ever become tame. This is where great patience really is a virtue.

5. Vomiting, coughing, or choking if more than occasionally.

6. Diarrhea or constipation. Blood-streaked fecal matter indicates a more serious complaint.

7. Swellings anywhere on the body.

8. Loss of spines.

9. Bald spots among the spines, or anywhere on the body. How-

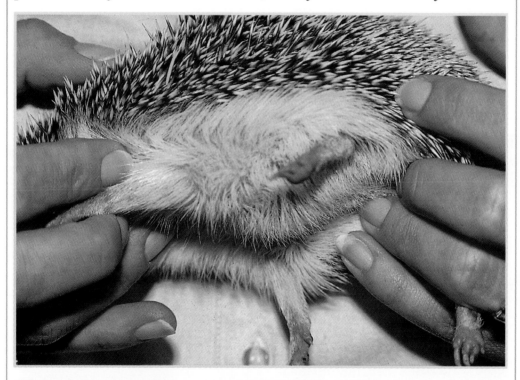

This female has a large lump on a mammary gland. Whether mastitis, abscess, or tumor, this hedgehog needs a veterinarian, not home doctoring or a first-aid kit.

The following are indicators of poor health:

1. Running eyes, or those which are not fully open when the hedgehog is wide awake.

2. Discharge of liquid from the nose. Swelling of one or both nostrils.

3. Foul-smelling ears (not common in these pets).

4. Labored or wheezy breathing.

ever, a narrow cranial median tract of no spines is normal.

10. Cuts and abrasions.

11. Flaky encrustations on the face, ears, underparts, or at the base of the spines.

12. Involuntary twitching of the body.

Before we discuss specific health problems, the subject of stress should be understood. It is possibly the singular most important precursor of ill health. Stress is not nervousness. An animal can be very nervous without being stressed. Conversely, a very stressed pet may not be at all nervous.

Stress may be defined as an animal's subconscious reaction to a missing need within the environment in which it lives. The more natural the omission, the greater the degree of stress. I would also link stress to intelligence insofar as those animals with a greater amount of intelligence appear to suffer more from stress than the less intelligent animals. However, this may simply be that the latter merely adjust more readily to the conditions that create stress.

Hedgehogs are not the most intelligent of animals; nonetheless they are predatory (albeit it on very small creatures) in their natural habitat. This implies enough intelligence for them to become stressed to a greater or lesser degree.

Because stress, unlike nervousness and other clinical signs, cannot be seen, it is difficult to pinpoint and treat. This fact also makes it difficult to say whether it has any hereditary basis. I rather suspect that it does. This may account for the fact that what may stress one individual may not do so to another.

If it cannot be seen, how do we know it exists? This has been established empirically over a number of years (especially with intensive farming methods) in much the same way that the science of genetics was appreciated long before it was possible to prove the theory of its actual mode of transmission.

Accepting its reality, it is not difficult to deduce the sort of conditions that will create stress and which stressors are likely to be especially prevalent in this animal.

1. Space: All animals need a given amount of space in which to move about. The less they have, the greater the effect of stress. Hedgehogs are very active creatures, so they must have plenty of exercise facility.

2. Foraging: Hedgehogs are natural foragers. Some of their food, such as dry cat biscuits, and even livefoods, should be scattered in their accommodations to enable them to utilize their scent and desire to seek food items via foraging. This provides psychological therapy.

3. Wallowing: Hedgehogs enjoy rolling in dust, soil, and their like. It is probably a means of eradicating parasites and possibly even helps in temperature control during very hot weather. To what degree it is a stressor under captive, thus controlled, conditions, is difficult to say, but it should not be ignored.

4. Inadequate Diet: If an important mineral or vitamin is missing in the diet, this may induce stress.

5. Noise: Hedgehogs are nocturnal. They venture out when it is relatively quiet. Excess noise and high-pitched sounds (electrical implements) are likely to induce stress.

Spine loss, flaky skin, and bald spots could indicate anything from a dietary deficiency to fungus to mites. A quick trip to the vet will tell for sure and the sooner treated the better.

6. Light: Avoid placing hedgehogs where they cannot escape intense direct light. Avoid startling hedgehogs by suddenly turning on lights. Leave a low-wattage light on in the room if you will be entering it after dark.

7. Handling: Even with very tractable hedgehogs, some will display a greater willingness to be handled than will others. Avoid excessive handling of an individual that clearly shows it wishes to be left alone—one that is wriggling a lot would be an example.

8. Interference: Waking up a sleeping pet regularly (as children are prone to do) will stress these timid animals.

9. Fear: Any animal placed in a situation where it is in real or believed danger from any implement, conspecific, or other animal, will become badly stressed. Do not allow other pets to continually harass your pet—dogs or cats pawing at it would be an example.

Bullying by another hedgehog sharing the same accommodations would fall under this heading. This is more likely if males are kept in close proximity (small cages) to each other.

10. Change of Ownership: This especially applies to a youngster about to leave the security of its mother and home. It is a very traumatic experience at a time when an infant is least able to cope in some ways.

THE CONSEQUENCES OF STRESS

Because many of the consequences of stress do have alternative sources, establishing stress as the causal agent is difficult. It can only be deduced if the other reasons are invalid. For example, your pet will scratch and bite its fur if it has parasites. If it does this for no reason, it falls under the heading of anomalous behavior.

Anomalies may be divided into various types, such as ingestive, aggressive, or reproductive. A few examples of these syndromes will indicate how dangerous they can be, and why they are precursors of ill health.

Ingestive: This ranges from eating fecal matter (coprophagia) to overeating (hyperphagia), thus obesity, to excessive drinking (polydipsia). It also includes hair eating (trichophagia). Within this category can also be included habits, such as excessive grooming to the point that abrasions are created, and bar biting, with resulting bruising of the snout and loss of teeth.

Aggressive: Butting with forehead, or upward jumping to spike the owner, biting, and ball curling are the three main examples, all of which, however, may have their source in temperament, and lack of proper socialization.

Reproductive: Inability of male to mate female (coital misalignment and low intromission effort), failure for sow to have correct estrus, cannibalism (partial or whole), rejection of offspring (abandonment), failure of sow to

A dense coat of spines is usually indicative of healthy skin.

Force feeding or administering oral medication is only possible with gentle, trusting hedgehogs.

let milk flow even if the newborns are accepted, and sporadic aggression toward offspring. Pacing around the cage for long periods of time should also be included in this list. (Alternatively, the condition may express itself in an almost total lack of movement, other than to eat).

OVERCOMING STRESS

In many instances, the only way to overcome existing stress is to rectify the causal problem, which assumes this has been reasonably deduced from the conditions the hedgehog is living under. However, certain stress conditions are not as easily overcome. They are habits internally reinforced by their very action.

Aggression is one example. It achieves an objective and becomes an integral part of a behavior pattern. Each time it is successful, it reinforces the behavior. Hyperphagia and polydipsia are other examples of internalized reinforcers. The very acts of eating and drinking are habit forming, especially the latter, given that hedgehogs should have ad lib water.

In this case, the answer is to change from a water bottle to an open dish. Part of the problem may be a licking syndrome (boredom induced) on the spout of inverted water dispensers. Hyperphagia will normally be limited to females in a colony system that is too small, or to pets that are given too much food, and too little space in which to live.

WHAT TO DO FIRST

Once you have ascertained that one or more of your hedgehogs is ill, in whatever form, a number of things must be done more or less concurrently. The nature of the problem will determine which, if not all, of the following are appropriate.

1. The hedgehog must be isolated from all other pets. This is your first job.

2. The pet must be placed in an environment that is very clean. This may necessitate a complete clean-out of the pet's housing and all furnishings and receptacles in it. Truthfully note the general level of cleanliness: you can deceive yourself, less so the vet, and never hard reality!

3. The temperature should be within the range discussed under housing, thus in the comfort zone.

4. The housing must be placed where the patient is not subject to noise or interference.

5. Supply clean fresh water if it is not already available.

6. Telephone your veterinarian after taking a few moments to make notes on the immediate case history and general living conditions. Your first reactive needs have now been completed.

PREPARING YOUR NOTES

1. Detail each sign of ill health and note when you first observed it. This establishes the progres-

One of the drawbacks to wood shavings as bedding is the likelihood of hedgehogs getting splinters in their face while rooting around. If you cannot remove them by hand or with tweezers, a visit to the vet is in order.

Maintaining proper light cycle, temperature, and body weight will prevent quite a few health problems. Education and good record keeping will also help.

sion of the problem. This may be characteristic of a given disease or ailment. Additionally, it will be useful to know the pet's weight and the state of its fecal matter—consistency and color.

2. Detail the conditions under which the pet is living. They should include the size and type (cage or open pen) of accommodations, temperature, other pets kept, diet, and if any other pets have recently been ill.

3. The immediate history will include information about how long you have owned the pet, where it was obtained, what its living conditions were like, and whether the pet has been taken anywhere (including outdoors) since you have owned it. Also include information about any previous medical treatments.

REVIEWING HUSBANDRY PRACTICE

At this time you should carefully review all of your husbandry practices, as discussed, to see if there are weak links in your methods, accommodations, diet, and environment. These matters must be rectified; otherwise, once the hedgehog is well, things may repeat themselves. If you are totally satisfied that all is as it should be, then it must be assumed that the problem arrived via airborne bacteria, via food, bedding, human or animal introduction, or their like.

PROBLEMS AND THEIR TREATMENT

The thrust of the text thus far has been directed at husbandry techniques and their importance. This cannot be overemphasized: the better the quality of husbandry, the easier it may be to pinpoint the cause of a problem.

Ailments will fall under two broad headings: external and internal. To them we can add injury, which will generally be of an external type—cuts or wounds. Successful treatment is based on an accurate diagnosis, but there are other considerations that you should be aware of.

With so many commercial drugs available these days, and under so many names, it can be all but impossible for you to decide which is best suited for treating the problem identified. The efficacy of one may not be nearly as good as another. Indeed, some may well eradicate one problem but create another because their constituents may be harmful to the hedgehog.

Reaction to drugs and dosages is based on extensive testing on a range of popular animals—dogs, cats, mice, rabbits and so on. When used on hedgehogs, at this time, there is a high degree of venturing into the unknown. Most are used in an extra label manner, meaning that they have not been approved for use on these pets. This would require very extensive research.

Additionally, physiological data on these pets is not readily available. That which is derives mainly from studies of the European species. While it is probable that such data will apply to *Atelerix,* the term probable implies a degree of uncertainty.

Given this background, you are strongly advised to seek veterinary advice when confronted with a problem. Even if specific information on diseases and drug reaction is limited, your vet is still far better able to make a judgment call than is anyone else.

EXTERNAL PARASITES

Hedgehogs may be parasitized by fleas, mites, and ticks. Of these, mites appear to be the most likely problem with domestic pets. Fleas are often species specific. Any that are seen on hedgehogs are possibly from another pet (dog, cat, rabbit). They will likely not survive for long. Nonetheless, if seen, owners will probably purchase flea powders or sprays, and may inadvert-

A properly set up hospital cage for sick animals should have solid, draft-free sides, an auxiliary heat source, and bedding that allows monitoring of fecal and urine output.

There are really very few tools required to properly tend to your hedgehog's health needs.

ently cause problems, even death, to the hedgehog. When using sprays, never allow the spray to enter the eyes or ears, and always follow the manufacturer's instructions.

Mites are slower moving than fleas and vary in size depending on their species. They may arrive via a number of means, and non-commercial wood shavings have been identified as one of them. Obtain only the proprietary branded shavings to minimize at least this route. Ticks are unlikely in pet hedgehogs (though widely seen on wild species) maintained within a home environment.

A wide range of ectoparasiticides is available and selection should take into account the following. The hedgehog has a considerable layer of subcutaneous fat that may absorb certain fat-soluble insecticidal chemicals. These substances are released slowly over a period of weeks as the fat layer is used and replaced (especially so in a torpid or unwell individual).

If additional insecticides are used, the result can be toxicity, the more so given the hedgehog's habit of self anointing (thus directly ingesting the toxins). Staley (1995) states that products containing synergists (compounds that inhibit cell enzyme actions in insects) should be avoided pending further data on their effect.

Specifically, N-octyl bicycloheptene dicarboxamide, when combined with pyrethrins, appears to have a very negative effect. It may even cause death, based on initial observations. At the least it may induce respiratory problems. Be sure to read the label carefully before purchasing any parasiticide.

It is important when selecting a parasiticide to use it exclusively, for better or worse, rather than changing brands on the pet during the same treatment period, or within the same environment. This means that you should not use one kind of product on the pet and a different one on its accommodations. If this is done, it may duplicate toxins, and makes assessment of side effects of the insecticide more difficult, if not impossible.

Adverse reaction to a treatment may be indicated by the pet twitching, having breathing problems, vomiting, or displaying convulsions. In such instances, as with any suspected poisons that may be on the spines or skin, the first priority is to remove them.

The hedgehog should be gently dipped into a shallow bowl of warm water (be sure it is not too hot). Do not allow water to get into its eyes or ears. Alternatively, stand the hedgehog in a bowl and use a spray to rinse it. After this is done, place the pet in a cozy box or carrier and take it to your vet for toxicological treatment.

Once a pet has been treated for parasites, its housing must be

The most frequently used tools will be nail clippers and styptic pencil. In captivity, hedgehogs don't wear their nails down, and they will have to be clipped.

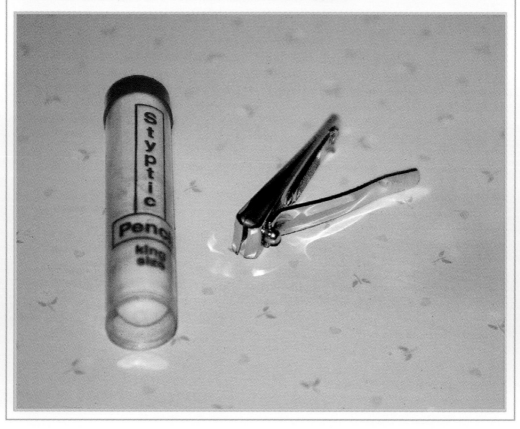

Allow the hedgehog to hide its head under one arm, grasp a foot firmly, and clip only the white portion, not the pink, which is the "quick," or vein, that runs through the nail.

thoroughly cleaned and treated as well. Remove and burn all bedding. A repeat treatment will be needed some days later in order to eradicate the hatched eggs that were not destroyed at the first treatment.

Should your pet have picked up a tick while being given exercise time in the garden, it will likely be seen in the head region but may be embedded between the spines of the neck or other parts. Do not pull the tick out before first placing chloroform, iodine, or a strong saline solution over the tick.

This will cause it to loosen its mouthparts, which are buried in the pet's skin. After a while, use tweezers to remove the tick(s) carefully, then treat the lesion with an antiseptic. The housing needs to be cleaned and treated for the eggs that may have been shed—burn all bedding material and replace it.

Maggots, which are the larvae of flies, can also be a problem. They may be found on lesions left unattended, or on the anal region of a hedgehog exhibiting diarrhea. They can be the source of many diseases. Unclean accommodations are a potential source. When present, maggots are best removed by flushing with a strong saline solution. After this is done, the lesion should be treated with an antiseptic ointment or lotion from your vet, who should inspect the wound if infestation was heavy.

INTERNAL PARASITES

Hedgehogs, like all higher animals, can be infested with a wide range of parasitic worms. At low levels, these worms do not present major problems, which arise with heavy infestations. Many require intermediate hosts such as snails, garden earthworms, insects, birds, reptiles, or mammals. These parasites include the following: nematodes (roundworms with unsegmented bodies), cestodes (tapeworms with false segmented bodies), and trematodes (flukes).

Discussion of individual species, in view of the potential number, serves little realistic purpose for the average hobbyist, who could not reliably identify them. More important is their effect and the ways they are identified and treated.

They parasitize the intestinal tract, organs such as the heart, liver, and lungs, and the blood. Some may not be evident as a causal agent until the individual dies and an autopsy is conducted. Others may cause characteristic symptoms. These include: vomiting, salivating, coughing, emaciation, loss of appetite, blood-streaked fecal matter, stunted growth, rapid breathing, pot belly, dry skin, loss of spines, lesions, coma, seizures, intestinal blockages, hemorrhage, and sudden death with no apparent cause.

Once a problem is apparent, your vet will do a fecal examination under low-power microscopy to assess the level of infestation. This may be expressed as eggs per gram (EPG) of fecal matter. Blood may also be screened for worms.

Fecal samples should ideally be fresh, and a number of them gathered for best analysis. They can be placed into a small plastic box or similar container.

Treatments are variable, with some having a broad range and others being more species specific. You are advised to obtain your anthelmintics (dewormers) from your vet, rather than another source. It is wise to have your vet conduct a worm egg count on breeding females some weeks prior to their being mated so that treatment, if needed, can be completed before the sow is bred.

You will note that many of the clinical signs of worms are the same as those for protozoan and fungal infections and diseases. For this reason, home diagnosis, or enlisting the counsel of an "I know the problem and can save you money" expert should be avoided.

It should also be added that topical treatments for dry skin and hair conditions are rarely worthwhile. Hair and spine "condition," as opposed to skin/spine problems, is internal. Correct diet is the key to fine skin, fur, and spine condition. Topical beauty aids merely mask an underlying problem.

FUNGAL INFECTIONS

Fungal infections can create many problems in hedgehogs, ranging from respiratory to gastro-intestinal, abortion to skin problems (ulcers), and spine loss. Fungi are mostly prevalent in soil, stagnant water, rotting vegetation, and unclean accommodations.

Some, such as ringworm, are zoonoses, meaning that they can be transferred to humans. Treatment is via various chemotherapeutics, such as polyene macrolide antibiotics, imidazoles, flucytosine, iodine and copper preparations to name but a few. Veterinary attention is required for both identification and recommended treatments.

Mycoses can be difficult to eradicate due to the resilience of spores to many treatments. Reinfection is not uncommon, so preventative husbandry, via cleanliness, is very important.

DIARRHEA

Many owners view this condition as a problem that can be treated as though it was a specific ailment. This is not the case. It is merely a clinical indicator of many conditions and diseases. It can indicate a very minor reaction to an excess of a given food, to incorrect diet, to parasites, or to a chill. Most of these conditions are self-limiting. However, diarrhea may be a symptom of a highly virulent disease. Only in combination with other clinical signs, microscopy of the fecal matter, and blood samples, can a diagnosis be made.

Nail clipping is best done on a slick surface where the hedgehog can't get any traction as he tries to run away. The hedgehog will wiggle, so keep a styptic pencil handy in case you cut into the quick.

When diarrhea is seen, the date should be noted, as well as the foods given in the previous 24 hours. If no other clinical signs are apparent, nor indication of abdominal pain, it is best to withhold foods for 24 hours. This should rectify the problem. If not, consult with your vet. Do not withhold water because diarrhea can rapidly dehydrate an animal.

Foods containing fats or dairy products will aggravate the condition, so if all appears better after 24 hours, introduce boiled chicken, and slowly return the diet to normal.

SALMONELLOSIS (SALMONELLA SPP)

The bacterial disease known as *salmonella* poisoning is discussed here not because it is prevalent in hedgehogs—quite the opposite—but in order to place the disease into perspective. The need to do so stems from an article that stated that hedgehogs can carry a bacterium called *Salmonella*, which could be transmitted to humans and cause diarrhea. Indeed it could, but this sort of article grossly misrepresents the full picture. It is an unfortunate reality within some magazine articles.

Salmonella is endemic worldwide. You may contract the condition from dogs, cats, horses, pigs, cattle, sheep, cage birds, poultry, goats, rabbits and other small pets, as well as from reptiles, amphibians, crustaceans, and all wild creatures.

Its source may be fouled water, food items, undercooked meats, meats that are not fresh, fecal matter, and handling diseased animals. To relate the disease to the hedgehog without stating that you are more likely to contract it from all of these other animals and pets, whose numbers far exceed those of hedgehogs, would seem to this author to be nothing short of unwarranted scaremongering.

Salmonella is a problem for *all* involved with animals—farmers, ranchers, stores selling fresh meat products, all pet breeders, as well as restaurants, hotels, and their like. By maintaining high standards of hygiene, you are no more likely to contract the problem from your hedgehog than from any other of the multifarious sources cited.

CONSTIPATION

This condition may result from foreign matter, hairs, small bones, hard skeletal tissue of insects, or other obstructions in the intestinal tract. It may also be the result of internal swellings, or other maladies of the rectal area. It may also follow diarrhea.

Very liquid feces, possibly blood-streaked, may bypass the blockage and suggest diarrhea. Abdominal palpation may indicate a swollen colon, whereby the hard fecal mass can be felt. Veterinary examination is needed because radiography may be required.

Minor constipation can be treated by oral administration of laxatives, such as mineral oil or dioctyl sodium sulfosuccinate, which help to break down the hard fecal matter. Gentle application of a lubricant to the anal area

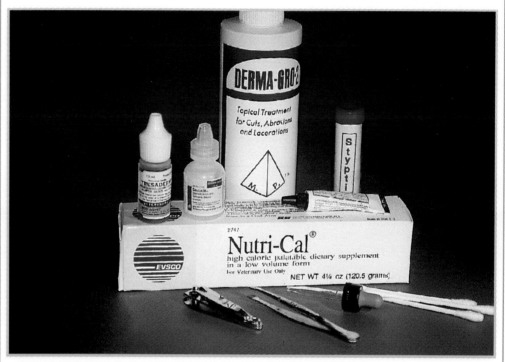

may help by making the skin softer. In severe cases, surgical removal of the blockage may be required. Routine use of laxatives is not recommended. Rather, the diet is the likely problem, so it is the means of correction.

DISEASE TREATMENTS

There is an impressive array of drugs available these days. Some have a wide spectrum of application, others are more specific. What is important for you to understand is that they have a

First aid supplies should be acquired before you need them. Experience is the best teacher so discuss with your vet the basics of first aid for your hedgehog.

DISEASES

The hedgehog can suffer from many of the diseases found in other mammals. At this time, there appear to be no major diseases that are especially associated with these insectivores. No doubt some will become so as the number of these pets increases, and studies made of them, their cause, and treatments. However, even so, their symptoms and effects will be much the same as already discussed in this chapter, as will their prophylaxis (prevention).

limited shelf life, and that all drugs may have adverse side effects, even when used as instructed.

Drugs are not always selective on the organisms that they kill. They may as readily destroy beneficial bacteria as well as those that are pathogenic. Their use therefore implies knowledge of dosage and duration of treatment if they are to be effective, yet have minimal side-effect risks. In some instances, they must be accompanied by vitamin treatment to replace those vitamins that are not being synthesized within the intestinal tract due to the effects of the medications on gut flora during treatment.

Drugs stored incorrectly may lose their efficacy, so always follow instructions as to dosage, length of treatment, storage and shelf life of these potentially dangerous compounds.

CUTS, WOUNDS, AND ABRASIONS

Hedgehogs are not especially prone to cuts or wounds because they will normally be living solitary lives within safe environments. However, during mating, fights can occur. Wounds to the ears, face, or underparts are the most likely sites for wounds.

Apart from blood loss in severe instances, the major risk is secondary infection by fungus or other pathogens (including worms and maggots). Once a wound is seen, the first thing to do is to assess its severity. If it is minor, it should be gently washed to remove any surface debris (shavings, dust, dirt). The application of an antiseptic lotion or cream should keep the lesion sterile while healing takes place. Check the wound daily.

If the wound is severe, the first thing to do is to apply a pressure bandage if this is possible. Should the bandage become soaked, apply another—do not remove the first one. If no pressure bandage is on hand, use any clean cotton or similar cloth that will stem the flow.

Avoid the use of tourniquets unless it is a real emergency. If too tight, they may adversely affect blood flow.

Needless to say, all but the most minor of wounds must be treated by a vet, as sutures may be required. In any case, there may be subcutaneous damage. The vet may also need to treat the pet for shock.

Hedgehogs kept in cages may claw at the bars and in so doing pull out or break a nail. This is not uncommon, but bleeding normally stops within a short period of time. However, it is a good idea to keep an eye on the nail, and maybe treat it with a tincture of iodine, potassium permanganate crystals, or a similar coagulant.

WOOD SHAVINGS

Like most owner/breeders, this author uses pine wood shavings as a bedding base for hedgehogs. Pine and cedar shavings are at this time receiving some adverse publicity (mostly from commercial sources that are marketing more expensive alternatives) that implicates the phenols and related compounds leached from them as being toxic to small mammals. They are said to have an adverse effect, over a period of time, on the respiratory, cardiac and other systems.

Phenol (carbolic acid) is used in disinfectants, and as an antiseptic. Its toxicity is determined by its relative concentration. Its effect as a disinfectant is to destroy the cellular structure of bacteria.

To what degree residual phenol compounds are active in commercially prepared shavings is open to much discussion. Further, neither the author nor the NAHA has seen any research material that relates to studies done on hedgehogs, which have a known high resilience to many compounds that would prove dangerous to other comparably sized mammals.

Until such time as verified data is available that indicates that the use of these woods is dangerous to these pets, we will continue to use them as being the most cost-efficient bedding, and one that might have beneficial side effects, as well as the claimed negatives.

One of the problems of modern living is that scientists are continually telling us what is dangerous, and offering us alternatives—only for other scientists to come along and point out the dangers in the alternatives! You must therefore make your own decision with regard to the use of shavings, pending more conclusive research one way or the other.

QUARANTINE

If you are a breeder, you should quarantine all newly acquired hedgehogs as far away from your main stock as possible. It would be wise to routinely have your vet do a worm egg flotation to establish this is within the safe zone. A powerful hand lens is useful for checking the skin for signs of parasites, especially mite action on the base of the spines and around the facial area.

The suggested isolation period is 14-21 days. This should be sufficient for any incubating problems to manifest themselves. During this period, monitor and adjust the diet as required, but do it gradually.

POSTMORTEM (AUTOPSY)

If a hedgehog should die for no diagnosed reason, it is wise to have your vet conduct an autopsy to see if some indication of cause of death can be established. The cost would be a sound investment for breeders because it may enable prevention of a recurrence.

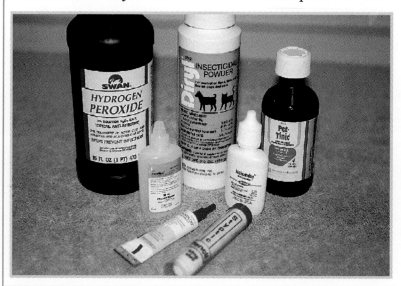

The products that you will need will vary, depending on whether you keep one pet or a breeding colony.

The North American Hedgehog Association (NAHA)

At the present time, the North American Hedgehog Association is in a state of flux because of reorganization efforts. Nevertheless, this chapter has been included in this book to provide historical documentation of the first, and possibly only, organization devoted to these fascinating little animals.

When a new pet hobby emerges, it goes through a number of stages. These stages are predictable, having been repeated time and again within different pets of past years. Once a pet is firmly established, and new mutations and varieties start to appear, its original evolutionary pattern repeats itself, but generally in a more controlled and acceptable manner.

The criteria as to whether a pet achieves popular status is determined by its ease of care, appeal, breeding potential, and so forth. Assuming these criteria are met, its ultimate popularity will be highly dependent on its hobby having a very active and high-profile national association to administer its needs.

Where pets do not have such associations, they will fail to achieve any lasting popularity, remaining within the realms of rare or exotic pets. Without a strong association, a pet hobby exists in a state of chaos, having no worthwhile direction, other

than to create money for those who prefer this situation to prevail.

The hedgehog hobby has been subject to all the forces discussed. It has reached that state where prices have fallen dramatically. Many of those whose sole object was to cash in on the pet have left the hobby. In their wake, they leave a trail of disaster for the serious hobbyists to correct. Fortunately for this pet, even while prices were high, an association was formed to address the hobby's future needs.

The North American Hedgehog Association came into being when Ralph Lermayer (President) of Bent, and Rod Frechette (Vice President) of Corrales, both in New Mexico, incorporated and funded the association's inception early in 1993.

In July 1993, a meeting of breeders convened in Denver, Colorado. Those present were noted in *African Pygmy Hedgehogs As Your New Pet* by this author (1994), so they need not be detailed here. The NAHA was not the only attempt by breeders to create a national association. A registry service was started in Texas, but it quickly disappeared, along with at least two breeder groups in other parts of the country.

The survival of any association is highly dependent on a number of factors coming together within a short time frame. The NAHA was fortunate in this respect, and it enabled the association to overcome early difficulties and firmly establish itself as the single national ruling body of the hobby.

In its president, it had a renowned photo journalist to help promote it. In its vice president, it had a highly successful Albuquerque attorney who gave it office and other administrative facilities. Within its initial membership, it had many of the most dedicated and respected breeders in the USA.

From a hobby perspective, the most readily available and lasting record of early pioneers and development comes via books. T.F.H. Publications was the first publisher to document the NAHA. In so doing, it added tremen-dously to the exposure of the NAHA, as it has done for other now well-established pet hobbies.

THE INITIAL OBJECTIVES

The NAHA created a three-tiered system for hobbyists. It published a magazine, *The Hedgehog News,* began a "Hobby Club Member" category, and started a "Registered Breeder" group. The objectives were to provide a source of sound advice to owners and breeders, to help change restrictive legislation, and to help provide a network of reputable breeders across the US.

The term "Hobby Club" was changed to "Member " in January 1995. During the same year, the magazine's name was changed to

The North American Hedgehog Association (NAHA) provides a newsletter to subscribers and members. The Hedgehog News *contains accurate, timely information for pet owners, breeders, and veterinarians.*

Hedgehog World International. This, it was felt, better reflected the long-term aspirations of the association.

The NAHA was successful in each of its defined areas. Hobbyists in numerous states, including New Mexico, Colorado, and Wyoming, to name but a few, may keep hedgehogs only because the association was able to persuade federal and state agencies to amend their policies to accommodate these pets.

It should be added that in so doing, a number of other mammalian pets, such as degus, sugar gliders, prairie dogs, spiny mice, and jerboas had their status clarified, and were added to the exempt list for pet shop and breeder sales. The association's beneficial activities have thus extended well beyond the hedgehog.

EXPANDED OBJECTIVES

The initial NAHA objectives were considerably expanded in 1994 when this author was appointed director of development. The new objectives became:

1. To draft a standard of excellence for the hedgehog, including the standardization of the colors, which had become a major source of confusion.

2. To appoint a panel of founder judges to draft the standard and pave the way for future judging appointments.

3. To introduce an affix system for breeder use and identification on pedigrees.

4. To create a national and international registration system as a means of tracing individual lineages of hedgehogs, and as a precursor for hedgehog exhibitions.

5. To help provide needed dispersal of veterinary information by implementing a program of bulletins specifically for veterinarians.

6. To develop a pet trade program that would further help pet shops to provide quality stock and sound information to their customers.

In January 1995, the administration of the association was transferred from Albuquerque to Nogal, New Mexico. During the same month, Ralph Lermayer stepped down as president due to time constraints. His office was taken by this author at the direction of Vice President Rod Frechette.

THE FOUNDER JUDGES

By the Spring of 1995, a panel of founder judges had been appointed. It included eminent pioneer breeders, together with breeders who had special skills and/or judging expertise within other pets, ranging from horses and dogs, to rabbits and guinea pigs. This was a historical landmark in the development of the hobby, so the judges, and their home states, are detailed herewith in the order of their appointment: Ralph Lermayer, New Mexico; Rod Frechette, New Mexico; Dennis Kelsey-Wood, New Mexico; Laura Lermayer, New Mexico; Dianne Campbell, Texas; Dawn Wrobel, Illinois; Stacey Storm, Washington; Kirsten Kranz, Wisconsin;

Valerie Stein, Oregon; Darin Kuhlow, Wisconsin; Richard Brisky, New York, Jan Erikson, Kansas; and Pat Storer, Texas.

Given the vast distances separating many of the judges, it is to their great credit that they were able to communicate and discuss the many complex issues before announcing what is the world's

You will see affixes and prefixes on the pedigrees of dogs, cats, horses, and most other major pets. The NAHA's system of application is somewhat different from most in that it was conceived to serve a more functional role than is usually the case. It is explained here so that you can better appreciate its value when viewing the

The first meeting of the NAHA brought together a group of concerned breeders whose first priority was to ensure the health and welfare of hedgehogs kept as pets.

first official standard of the domestic hedgehog, *Atelerix albiventris,* the African pygmy hedgehog.

THE NAHA AFFIX SYSTEM

An affix is a name allocated to an individual breeder. It is registered with the national ruling body so that it can be affixed to the name of a hedgehog on a pedigree to denote the breeder.

pedigree of a NAHA-registered hedgehog, or its lineage.

First of all, the NAHA grants an affix only to registered breeders. This is to avoid a situation in which pedigrees are unduly cluttered with the prefixes and affixes of what may be termed occasional breeders. A NAHA affix denotes that its owner is a very serious hobbyist who maintains at least certain basic standards of care and hygiene that are regulated by the USDA, and monitored by their inspectors. Only holders of a USDA license may apply for registered breeder status.

Apart from this requirement, the NAHA also applies other rules to this group of breeders, but they need not be detailed here. The objective is to maintain, as far as possible, certain standards of practice and ethics that are conducive to the best welfare of hedgehogs, and to serving those who own or are seeking to obtain one. It immediately tells you that the breeder is well informed on this pet in all areas of its management.

An affix is applied after the name of the hedgehog and will always be preceded by "of." It indicates the *breeder* of the hedgehog. For example, Tinkerbelle of Avalon indicates that this female was bred by the Lermayers, to whom this affix is registered.

If an affix holder purchases another breeder's hedgehog, he can use his own affix as a prefix to denote that he owns that hedgehog but did not breed it. For example, the female mentioned above was purchased by this author, who holds the affix of Camelot. She is registered as Camelot's Tinkerbelle of Avalon. An affix used as a prefix is therefore always in the possessive: it indicates that the present owner is a registered breeder.

If a non-registered breeder obtains a hedgehog from an affix holder, this information should thereafter be denoted on a pedigree by an asterisk appearing before the animal's name, e.g., *Houdini of Cheredzi. All other names on a NAHA pedigree that have no affix or prefix are owned/bred by non-registered breeder members of the association.

For the purpose of providing a historical perspective, the first eighteen affixes registered in the USA are given here. Many will be seen on the pedigrees of future breeders' foundation stock. The complete list is published annually by the association, as well as on registered breeder listings.

THE FIRST 18 AFFIXES IN THE USA

AintNoCreek, Dawn Wrobel, Illinois

Avalon, Ralph/Laura Lermayer, New Mexico

Bon-Art, Bonnie Bogart, Colorado

Camelot, Dennis/Eve Kelsey-Wood, New Mexico

Cedar Park, Claudette A. Parker, Oklahoma

Cheredzi, Dianne Campbell, Texas

Hedgehog Heaven, Rod/Michelle Frechette, New Mexico

High Meadow, Sharon Rock, Washington

Hinestein Exotics, Valerie Stein, Oregon

Kuhl, Darin Kuhlow, Wisconsin

Overland, Dorothy/Ben Bath, Colorado

Ozark Ridge, Beth O'Neil, Illinois

Prickle Bush, Kirsten Kranz, Wisconsin

Rosebud, Pam Howard, Illinois

RZU-2U, Pat Storer, Texas

Spiny Holler, Ena Stackhouse, North Carolina

The NAHA also offers great merchandise like T-shirts and bumper stickers.

Members of the North American Hedgehog Association dispense information at many gatherings of pet owners and exotic-animal breeders.

Sweetwater, Richard Brisky, New York

Triple "O", Stacey Storm, Washington

THE VETERINARY PROGRAM

The hedgehog has presented many veterinarians with somewhat of a problem arising from lack of information. Indeed, some owners have found that their vet is disinclined to attempt treatments for anything but the most minor of conditions. This prompted the association to commence gathering as much veterinary-appropriate information as it could, and to dispense this information only to veterinarians via a number of bulletins.

HEDGEHOG EXHIBITIONS

With the forthcoming presentation of hedgehog exhibition events, the full evolution of the hedgehog from a collection of wild imports to a major pet hobby will have been completed. The NAHA is dedicated to the ongoing welfare of hedgehogs and to serving the needs of all who have found these adorable, unusual, and challenging mammals to be everything they had hoped for in an exotic pet.

An interesting feature of the NAHA shows will be that, apart from the regular show classes based on conformation and colors, they will also feature habitat classes. These classes will enable pet owners, as well as dedicated breeders, to display interesting mini habitats to show the very many design ideas that can be incorporated into hedgehog accommodations.

For readers in any country who wish to join the association or to learn more about it, address inquiries to: NAHA, PO Box 122, Nogal, New Mexico, 88341, USA.

Appendix

UNITED STATES DEPARTMENT OF AGRICULTURE (USDA) LICENSING INFORMATION

The Animal Welfare Act became law in 1966. Its objective is to ensure that animals are maintained under healthy, regulated conditions and treated humanely. If you are planning to breed hedgehogs that will be sold to others as breeding stock, you are required to be licensed. The selling of hedgehogs to someone who is going to sell them will also require licensing.

To obtain a license, contact your sector USDA Animal and Plant Inspection Service (APIS) and request an information package, along with a registration application form. Return the completed form with the appropriate fee and, in due course, an inspector will visit your premises. Once you have been granted a license, you will be charged a scaled annual fee based on your sales. It is not excessive.

SECTOR OFFICES

North Central Sector: Illinois, Indiana, Iowa, Minnesota, Michigan (Upper Peninsula), Wisconsin, N. Dakota, S. Dakota, Nebraska USDA, APHIS, Butler Square West, Room 625, 100 North Sixth St., Minneapolis, MN 55403, (612) 370-2255

Northeast Sector: Connecticut, Delaware, District of Columbia, Maine, Maryland, Massachusetts, Michigan (Lower Peninsula), New Hampshire, New Jersey, New York, Ohio, Pennsylvania, Rhode Island, Vermont, West Virginia USDA, APHIS, 2568-A Riva Road, Suite 302, Annapolis, MD 2140-7400, (301) 962-7463

South Central Sector: Arkansas, Kansas, Louisiana, southern Mississippi, Missouri, Oklahoma, Texas USDA, APHIS, 501 Felix Street, PO Box 6258, Fort Worth, TX 76115, (817) 885-6923

Southeast Sector: Alabama, Florida, Georgia, Kentucky, northern Mississippi, N.Carolina, Puerto Rico, S.Carolina, Tennessee, Virginia, Virgin Islands USDA, APHIS, 501 East Polk Street, Suite 820, Tampa, FL 33602, (813) 225-7690

Western Sector: Alaska, Arizona, California, Hawaii, Idaho, Montana, Nevada, New Mexico, Oregon, Utah, Washington, Wyoming USDA, APHIS, 9580 Micron Avenue, Suite E, Sacramento, CA 95827, (916) 551-1561

References and Bibliography

The following list of references and books is selective. It is based on articles cited in the text, others which will be of interest to serious hobbyists, and books consulted for facts and opinions.

Brockie, R. 1974. "Self-anointing in wild hedgehogs, *Erinaceus europaeus,*" *New Zealand Animal Behavior,* 24: 68-71.

Brodie, Edmund D., III, Brodie, Edmund D., Jr., and Johnson, Judith A. 1982. "Breeding the African hedgehog *Atelerix pruneri* in captivity,"*Int. Zoo Yearbook,* Vol. 22, 195-197.

Brodie, Edmund D, Jr. 1977. "Hedgehogs use toad venom in their own defense," *Nature,* Vol. 268, 5621:627-628.

Corbet, G.B. 1988. "The family Erinaceidae: a synthesis of taxonomy, phylogeny, ecology, and zoogeography," *Mammalian Review,* 18:117-72.

Crandall, Lee S. 1964. *The Management of Wild Animals in Captivity,* Families Tenricidae (sic) and Erinaceidae, pp46-48, University of Chicago Press, Chicago and London.

Gregory, M. 1976. "Notes on the central African hedgehog *Erinaceus albiventris* in the Nairobi area," *E. Afr. Wildl. Journ.,* 14:177-179.

Grzimek, H.C.B. Editor. 1976. *Encyclopedia of Evolution,* Van Nostrand Reinhold, New York, NY.

Jones, M.L. 1982. "Longevity of captive animals," *Zoo Garten,* 52:113-28.

Kelsey-Wood, Dennis. 1994. *African Pygmy Hedgehogs As Your New Pet,* T.F.H. Publications, Inc., Neptune, NJ, 1995.

Kelsey-Wood, Dennis. 1995. "Ecosystems—the alternative housing, part one," *The Hedgehog News,* 1995:1.

Kelsey-Wood, Dennis. 1995. "Ecosystems—the alternative housing, part two," *Hedgehog World International,* 1995:2, North American Hedgehog Assoc., Inc., Nogal, NM.

Kranz, Kirsten 1995. "Hand-raising newborns: yes, it can be done!" *Hedgehog News,* 1995:1, North American Hedgehog Assoc.Inc., Nogal, NM.

Machin, Dr. K. and Wheler, Dr. C. 1995. "Hedgehogs not such easy pets," *The Star Phoenix,* April 24, Saskatoon, SK, Canada.

Mayr, Ernst. 1969. *Principles of Systematic Zoology,* McGraw-Hill Co., New York and London.

Merck Veterinary Manual. 1991. 7th edition, Merck & Co., Inc. Rahway, NJ.

Nowak, Ronald M. 1991. *Walker's Mammals of the World.* 5th edition, Vol. 1., pp114-138, Order Insectivora, Johns Hopkins University Press, Baltimore and London.

Robins, C.B. and Setzer, H.W. 1985. "Morphometrics and distinctiveness of the hedgehog genera (Insectivora: Erinaceidae), *Proc. Biol. Soc.,* Washington, 98:112-120.

REFERENCES AND BIBLIOGRAPHY

Scientific Tables, 1970. 7th edition, Ciba-Geigy Ltd., Basle, Switzerland.

Smith, DVM, Anthony J. 1992. "Husbandry and medicine of African hedgehogs (*Atelerix albiventris*)," *Journal of Small Exotic Animal Medicine*, 2:21-26.

Staley, DVM, E.C. 1994. "Hedgehog health and husbandry: ectoparasite control." *The Hedgehog News*, Number Two, North American Hedgehog Assoc. Inc., Albuquerque, NM.

Staley, DVM, E.C. 1995. "Hedgehog health and husbandry: adverse reaction to insecticide," *The Hedgehog News*, 1995:1, North American Hedgehog Assoc., Inc., Nogal, NM.

Stocker, L. 1987. *The Complete Hedgehog*. Chatto & Windus, London.

Storer, Pat. 1994. *Everything You Wanted to Know About Hedgehogs But You Didn't Know Who to Ask*. 3rd edition. Country Storer Enterprises, Columbus, Texas.

United States Department of Agriculture (USDA), 1992. Licensing and registration under the Animal Welfare Act. Program Aid 1117, Regional Animal Care Sector Offices.

Walker, 1991. *See* Nowak, Ronald M.

Wrobel, Dawn. 1995. "Cannibalism & abandonment in hedgehogs," *The Hedgehog News*, 1995:1, North American Hedgehog Assoc., Inc., Nogal, NM.

Index

INDEX